PON

MW01109391

OUR

FAITH

Faith Formation Basics
for faithful followers
of Jesus the Christ
to learn, teach, and pray

With traditional songs, pastoral notes and reflection questions,
for adults, parents, catechists, & faith sharing groups, compiled
around excerpts from the *National Directory for Catechesis*
of the *United States Conference of Catholic Bishops*, 2005

Compiled by
Stephen Joseph Wolf

idjc press

Excerpts from the *National Directory for Catechesis,* copyright 2005,
United States Conference of Catholic Bishops, Washington, D.C.
Reprinted with permission. All rights reserved.

Scripture texts used in this work are taken from the *New American
Bible,* copyright 1991, 1986, and 1970 by the Confraternity of Christian
Doctrine, Washington, DC 20017 and are used by permission of the
copyright owner. All rights reserved.

Pondering Our Faith was originally compiled by Rev. Steve Wolf
as *Faith Formation Basics* for the *FIAT (Faith In Action Together)
Groups* of St. Stephen Catholic Community in
Hermitage, Old Hickory, & Mt. Juliet,
and completed while serving as Associate Pastor of
St. Henry Church in Nashville, Tennessee.

Cover art *Mary* is by Mary Borgen,
Joseph, Trinity and *Jesus* (details) are by Keith Tucker,
and *Alleluia* is by Stephen Joseph Wolf.

Printed in the U.S.A. and distributed by Ingram Books
Published by idjc press; contact at steve@idjc.info

ISBN 978-0-9795549-5-7

Additional copies are available from
St. Mary's Bookstore in Nashville, Tennessee
www.stmarysbookstore.com
www.amazon.com
and other fine bookstores.

Any attempt to articulate the faith will be imperfect,
because we are talking here about our God.

The weekly "background" of *Pondering Our Faith* is
drawn from the 2005 document of the U.S. Bishops,
National Directory of Catechesis,
which comes from input by countless faithful,
clergy and lay, in a brave attempt of this generation
to articulate the Christian faith.

Thanks be to all who participated in that process.

Nicene Creed

We believe in one God, the Father, the Almighty,
maker of heaven and earth, of all that is seen and unseen.

We believe in one Lord, Jesus Christ,
the only Son of God,
eternally begotten of the Father,
God from God, Light from Light,
true God from true God,
begotten, not made, one in Being with the Father.
Through him all things were made.
For us men and for our salvation
he came down from heaven:
by the power of the Holy Spirit
he was born of the Virgin Mary and became man.
For our sake he was crucified under Pontius Pilate;
he suffered, died and was buried.
On the third day he rose again
in fulfillment of the Scriptures;
he ascended into heaven
and is seated at the right hand of the Father.
He will come again in glory
to judge the living and the dead,
and his kingdom will have no end.

We believe in the Holy Spirit, the Lord, the giver of life,
who proceeds from the Father and the Son.
With the Father and the Son he is worshiped and glorified.
He has spoken through the Prophets.

We believe in one holy catholic and apostolic Church.
We acknowledge one baptism for the forgiveness of sins.
We look for the resurrection of the dead,
and the life of the world to come. Amen.

PONDERING OUR FAITH

Members of **faith sharing groups** are encouraged to bring their favorite Bible to weekly meetings; follow the opening passages in your Bible as you hear them read.

If you read this book **on your own**, you will get much more from it by beginning each chapter with the short passages indicated from your own Bible.

Group Process

Are you in a faith sharing group?

Our faith is a living faith, alive in history, ever ancient and ever new, rooted in the mission that Jesus Christ entrusted to the first apostles: *to proclaim his Gospel and bring people into communion with God.* NDC, page 3

We have but to read the ancient psalms, or any ancient literature, to know that our core identity does not change, nor does our God. Still, most generations think that their predicament is unique in human history. This is true, in that each human being is created uniquely in God's image, like none before exactly, like none to come. Our faith does not change, but sometimes a particular way that we articulate our faith does develop. This presentation of the faith for our generation is drawn from the 2005 *National Directory for Catechesis* published by the U.S. Conference of Catholic Bishops, following the 2002 *General Directory for Catechesis* from the Congregation for the Clergy for the universal Church. I enjoy being challenged by it, and hope that you will too, remembering that Christ entrusts his mission to his Church of seekers, disciples, ministers, and, yes, you apostles.

Pondering Our Faith was compiled for faith sharing in groups over six weekly meetings. Some will naturally prefer to read this on their own, and that is fine. Even for those in a group setting, it can often be helpful to read and reflect on our own beforehand, especially if there are any unhealed experiences of life or faith. I have heard many people name the Church as the locus for the hurt of their lives. As priests are so often called to do, I offer my heartfelt apology, with the Church, universal and Catholic. I invite those who carry an unhealed wound to bring that hurt into these reflections, and ask the Lord to lead you to a person of faith with whom you can safely tell your story.

Possible Group Ground Rules

Faith Sharing is:

REGULAR: I will do my best to make all sessions.

DISCERNED: There is no need to answer every question. Questions are offered to prompt sharing of stories. It is acceptable to simply offer an observation.

VOLUNTARY: No one is required to share. The tone is invitational. Verbal participation is encouraged but not demanded.

NOT INTERRUPTED: When someone is sharing, everyone listens before commenting or speaking. Side conversations are avoided; one person at a time.

NOT CONTRADICTED: The sharing is based on the person's own life story, so conclusions or critiques of what is shared are not appropriate. Avoid trying to take away feelings with comments like, *You shouldn't feel that way.*

DONE IN "I" LANGUAGE: beginning with *I think* or *I feel* rather than *Mary said* or *Joe thinks.*

CONFIDENTIAL: What is said in the group stays in the group.

(These ground rules are drawn from Joye Gros' *Theological Reflection,* Loyola Press, 2002. Groups are free to alter them as they wish.)

_____
I agree with the group ground rules.   (Signature and Date)

Ephesians 1:   Blessed Be

Melody: *Joyful, Joyful, We Adore Thee…*

Bless-ed be the God and Fa-ther
of our Lord_ Je-sus Christ,
Who has blessed us in the Christ_,
bless-ings in their Spir-it breath.
As God chose us in the Mes-si-ah
be-fore_ found-ing sky or earth,
To be ho-ly, clean of blem-ish,
in God's eye: a-dop-tion worth.

In the Son we have re-demp-tion,
God's for-give-ness of our sin,
By the rich-es of his grace_
lav-ished on us, gath-ered in.
Giv-ing wis-dom, know-ledge_, vi-sion,
mys-t'ry_ of the Fa-ther's will,
Sum-ming up all things in Je-sus,
fa-vored in the full-ness sent.

In our hear-ing of the gos-pel
word of our sal-va_-tion,
One by one we too were cho-sen,
•   joined as part-ners with the Son.
By the prom-ised Ho-ly_ Spir-it,
signed and_ sealed as heirs of God,
God's pos-se-sion, God's re-demp-tion,
God's be-lov-ed, Ab-ba's own.

Text: from Ephesians 1:3-14, New American Bible, by Stephen J. Wolf, 2008
         with gratitude to the Institute for Priestly Formation
Music: HYMN TO JOY 8787D, Ludwig van Beethoven, 1770-1827;
         Adapted by Edward Hodges, 1796-1867

1

THE NEW EVANGELIZATION

Opening Prayer: The Nicene Creed (see page iv) all together.

Review together Possible Group Ground Rules. (see page 3)

A member of the group reads   **1 Timothy 2:1-7**
while others read along in their Bibles.

A member of the group reads   **Luke 5:1-11**
while others read along in their Bibles.

Then group members take turns reading the background:
(NDC, page 47)

The **new evangelization** is primarily the 'clear and unequivocal proclamation of the person of Jesus Christ, that is, the preaching of his name, his teaching, his life, his promises and the Kingdom which he has gained for us by his Paschal Mystery.'EA66 It involves the active participation of every Christian in the proclamation and demonstration that the Christian faith is the fully valid response to the problems and hopes that life poses to every person and society.CL34 *

Footnote references are provided in full on pages 102-104.

The new evangelization is directed [first] to the Church herself:

[1] to [those] baptized who [have not yet been] effectively evangelized…,

[2] to those who have [not] made a personal commitment to Christ and the Gospel,

[3] to those formed by the values of the…culture,

[4] to those who have lost a sense of faith, and

[5] to those who are alienated.

[The new evangelization] is also directed to all human cultures so that they might be open to the Gospel and live in harmony with Christian values. SD22   The new evangelization is aimed at personal transformation through the development of a personal relationship with God, participation in sacramental worship, the development of a mature ethical and social conscience, ongoing catechesis, and a deepening integration of faith into all areas of life.

…Faith [and conversion involve] …a profound change of mind and heart, a change of life, [in Greek] a "*metanoia*." EN10 Such a change can only arise from deep within the interior of one's being, where one faces the truly important questions about human life. Such a change, engendered by the Holy Spirit, shows itself in the transformation of one's life.

Yet I live, no longer I, but Christ lives in me.
Saint Paul, Galatians 2:20

God's Self-Disclosure

'It pleased God, in his goodness and wisdom, to reveal himself and to make known the mystery of his will.'DV2 The divine will is that we should come to the Father through Christ, the Word made flesh, and, in the Holy Spirit, become sharers in the divine nature (*theosis*). Divine Revelation, then, is the supernatural manifestation [showing forth] of the inner life of God: Father, Son, and Holy Spirit. God's desire to communicate himself to us is entirely his own initiative. God's self-revelation aims to bring about our participation in the life of the Blessed Trinity, something so wondrous that it is impossible for us even to imagine.

From the beginning, God has made known the inexhaustible mystery of his love in order to give us a share in his own divine life. In doing so, God summons a response in faith from his people. So unimaginable is God's gift of himself that our response can only be self-surrender, the obedience of faith. God reveals himself to us gradually and in stages, drawing us ever closer in order to prepare us to welcome the culmination of God's self-revelation in the person and mission of the incarnate Word, Jesus Christ. The pattern of this Revelation unfolds through 'deeds and words, which are intrinsically [connected]: . . . the works performed by God in the history of salvation show forth and bear out the doctrine and realities signified by the words; the words, for their part, proclaim the works, and bring to light the mystery they contain.'DV2

God first revealed himself through creation and continually provides evidence of himself in the created

7

order. God sustains and directs creation toward its fulfillment in Jesus Christ. God revealed himself in a special way through the history of Israel.JP19-65 [God] created our first parents in communion with him. After their fall, he revealed his loving plan for redemption through covenants with Noah and Abraham. In the time of the patriarchs, Isaac, Jacob, and Joseph, he formed Israel as his people so that they would know the one, true God. God freed the Israelites from slavery in Egypt, established the covenant of Mount Sinai, and, through Moses, gave them his law. He spoke to his people through judges, priests, and prophets and continued to shape his people in hope for the promised Savior. God made a covenant with King David and promised that through David's offspring, he would establish his kingdom for ever. (Cf.2Sm 7:13) We see this covenant promise fulfilled in Mary, the virgin mother of God's only-begotten Son. She was a unique vessel of God's Revelation, obediently bringing forth his Word in human flesh in order to establish...[the] kingdom [of God] for ever.

God revealed himself fully in Jesus Christ, the Son of God made man. Jesus is the 'mediator and the sum total of Revelation.'DV2 In Christ, God has said everything in one, perfect, transcendent Word. Jesus Christ 'completed and perfected Revelation. ...He did this by the total fact of his presence and self-manifestation - by words and works, signs and miracles, but above all by his death and glorious resurrection from the dead, and finally by sending the Spirit of truth.'DV4 There will be no new public revelation until Christ returns in glory at the end of time.

God is that of which no greater can be thought.　St. Anselm

8

God's Revelation is intended for all [of] humanity because God 'wills everyone to be saved and to come to knowledge of the truth.'(1 Tim 2:4) To fulfill this divine plan, Jesus Christ founded the Church on the apostles, filled them with the Holy Spirit, and sent them to preach the Gospel to the whole world. This apostolic commission has been the life of the Church since her foundation. The Church has preserved the integrity and entirety of the Gospel since Christ entrusted it to her. The Gospel has been the source of her inspiration, the object of her contemplation, the subject of her proclamation, and the reason for her missionary activity. 'The integral conservation of Revelation, the word of God contained in Tradition and Scripture, as well as its continuous transmission, are guaranteed in their authenticity'GDC44 by the Holy Spirit.

Through Tradition, 'the Church, in her doctrine, life and worship, perpetuates and transmits to every generation all that she herself is, all that she believes.'DV8 Handing on Divine Revelation to future generations of believers is a principal work of the Church under the guidance of the Holy Spirit. Christ commanded the apostles to preach the Gospel, which he himself proclaimed, and which he fulfilled in his own person. They did so through their own preaching, their example, and the institutions they established. They also communicated what they had seen and heard in writing, under the inspiration of the Holy Spirit. These sacred books held the message of salvation that Christ entrusted to them and that they were to safeguard until the end of time. 'In order that the full and living Gospel might always be preserved in the church, the apostles left bishops as their successors. They gave them *their own position of teaching authority.*'DV7

By the power of the Holy Spirit, Christ must be proclaimed to every person and to all nations in every age so that God's Revelation may reach the ends of the earth.

> *God, who spoke in the past, continues to converse with the spouse of his beloved Son [the Church]. And the Holy Spirit, through whom the living voice of the Gospel rings out in the Church - and through her in the world - leads believers to the full truth, and makes the Word of Christ dwell in them in all its richness.*DV8

God's self-revelation given through his only Son in the Holy Spirit remains living and active in the Church. Sacred Tradition and Sacred Scripture together are the **Deposit of Faith**, which is guarded and protected by the Magisterium because it was given to us by Christ and cannot change. The transmission of that Revelation, in its integrity, is entrusted, by Divine Commission, to the Magisterium, to the Successor of St. Peter and the Successors of the Apostles. In a harmonious collaboration with the Magisterium in the Church's mission of evangelization, all the members of the People of God, priests, deacons, men and women religious, and the lay faithful, hand on the faith by proclaiming the Good News of salvation in Jesus Christ and communicating God's gift of his own divine life in the sacraments.

> (Pastoral note: While the deposit of faith does not change, the manner in which it is transmitted can develop in history.)

10

Faith
(NDC page 45)

From the beginning, God has made known the inexhaustible mystery of his love in order to give us a share of his own divine life. In doing so, God summons a response in faith from his people, a response that itself is a gift. …[Our] response can only be self-surrender, the obedience of faith (Cf. Romans 16:26), of which Mary is the perfect embodiment.

Human beings are unique in creation because they alone can offer God a response of faith to his initiative of love. The response of faith has two integral dimensions: the faith *by which* one believes and the faith *which* one believes. Faith is a supernatural virtue. Faith is one's personal adherence to God who reveals himself; at the same time, faith is the free assent of one's intellect and will to the whole Truth that God has revealed.Cf.CCC150 The faith *by which* one believes is itself a gift from God. It is God's grace that moves and assists the individual to believe. It is the interior help of the Holy Spirit that moves the heart and converts it to God.Cf.DV5 The faith *which* one believes is also God's gift. It consists of the content of Divine Revelation. Faith, then, is the human response to a [self-revealing] personal God, and to the Truth that God has revealed through the…Church.

Whatever can be known or understood is less than God.
St. Thomas Aquinas

(When we speak of God, as we must,)
in whatever similarity, there is an even greater dissimilarity.
Fourth Lateran Council

11

Conversion

'The Christian faith is, above all, conversion to Jesus Christ.'GDC15;Cf.JDDJ16 It is the fruit of God's grace and the free response to the prompting of the Holy Spirit. It arises from the depths of the human person and involves such a profound transformation of heart and mind that it causes the believer to change radically both internally and externally. The Blessed Virgin Mary's perfect response to the grace of the Holy Spirit represents the primordial conversion to Christ and the 'purest realization of faith.' CCC149...

The process of conversion involves understanding who Christ is [and the grace to be changed and] follow him more closely. Conversion begins with an openness to the initial proclamation of the Gospel and a sincere desire to listen for its resonance within. This search arouses in those coming to Christ a desire to know him more personally and to know more about him. This knowledge of the person, message, and mission of Christ enables the believer to 'make it into a living, explicit and fruitful confession of faith.'GDC82 This profession of faith forms the foundation for the continuing journey under the guidance of the Holy Spirit. It is nourished by the sacraments, prayer, and the practice of charity 'until we all attain to the unity of faith and knowledge of the Son of God . . . to the extent of the full stature of Christ.' (Eph 4:13)

> 'This is crucial: ...be converted -
> ...continue to be converted!
> ...let the Holy Spirit change our lives!
> ...respond to Jesus Christ.' GMD14

12

The Good News of Salvation

(NDC, page 79)

[We can emphasize] several basic points that Jesus made throughout his preaching:

1. God is a loving Father who abides with his people.

2. With the coming of the kingdom,
   [a] God offers us salvation,
   [b] frees us from sin,
   [c] brings us into communion with him and all
       humanity, and
   [d] promises eternal salvation.

3. The Kingdom of God is one of justice, love, and peace, in the light of which we shall be judged.

4. The Kingdom of God is inaugurated in the person of Jesus Christ Cf.LG3; it is in mystery present now on the earth and will be perfected when the Lord returns.

5. The Church, the community of disciples,
   [a] 'is, on earth, the seed and the beginning of that
       kingdom'LG5 and
   [b] 'is effectively and concretely at the service of the
       Kingdom.'RM20

6. The Church offers a foretaste of the world to come...

[7.] [And] human life is a journey...to God.

Trinity
(NDC, page 91)

God is Father, Son, and Holy Spirit: one God in three divine persons. The inner life of the Trinity and the actions of the divine persons are undivided and inseparable. Who God is and what he does form a unity of divine life and activity. The work of Revelation is the common work of the three divine persons. Each person of the Trinity, however, shows forth what is proper to him within the one divine nature. Therefore, the Church confesses 'one God and Father **from** whom all things are, and one Lord Jesus Christ, **through** whom all things are, and one Holy Spirit **in** whom all things are.' (Council of Constantinople II, no.421, emphases added) These properties of the divine persons within the Trinity are reflected in the pedagogy of God.

Pastoral note: "Pedagogy of God" refers to God's own methodology, God's way of teaching us.

If you understand it, it is not God you are understanding.
St. Augustine

14

Father
(NDC, page 91)

The Father made himself known in creation and in his eternal Word, Jesus Christ. Through the mystery of the incarnation, Jesus revealed God as Father and Creator: the eternal Father of his only-begotten Son and the Creator of all that exists. Out of nothing [ex nihilo] and through his eternal Word and Spirit, the Father created all things, and all creation is good. By his Word, who is his perfect image from all eternity, his 'Son,' the Father upholds and sustains the whole creation; he both transcends his creation and is present within it.

The Father bestowed his word on generation after generation of believers until in the fullness of time he [spoke] his one unsurpassable Word in the person of Jesus Christ. He made a covenant with his people that bound him to them and them to him in an everlasting pledge of love, liberating them from the bondage of slavery and sin. He transformed events in the life of his people into encounters with himself. He formed his people through victory and defeat, reward and punishment, happiness and sorrow, forgiveness and suffering. [God the Father gave the Law to the Chosen People through Moses.] The moral law that derives from it 'can be defined as fatherly instruction.'CCC1950 He showed himself throughout the history of Israel in many manifestations, 'in which the cloud of the Holy Spirit both revealed him and concealed him in its shadow.'CCC707

Pastoral note: We use the masculine word "Father" as Jesus asked us to, which can be very helpful in building a personal relationship with God. A warning: it can also let us think we have God figured out. This I find helpful: God is neither masculine nor feminine, God is both masculine and feminine, God is beyond masculine or feminine...

Jesus Christ

(NDC, page 92)

Jesus Christ...became **truly human** while remaining **truly God**. God's eternal Word became flesh to help us know God's love, to save us, to be our model of holiness, and to have us 'share in the divine nature.'(2Ptr1:4) In the mystery of his incarnation, Christ joins divinity with humanity in teaching the faith and forming disciples.

Christ's relationship with his disciples also reveals God's [ways]… In a sign of basic human affirmation, Jesus chose his apostles; they did not choose him.(Cf.Jn15:16) He established a bond of friendship with them that was the context for his teaching. 'I have called you friends,' he said, 'because I have told you everything I have heard from my Father.'Jn15:15 He engaged them in lively conversations by asking them probing questions: 'Who do people say that I am?' Mk8:27 He gave them hope: when they saw him coming toward them on the water, he said, 'Take courage, it is I, do not be afraid!'Mk6:50 After he taught the crowds, he explained the meaning of his teaching to his disciples 'in private.'Mk4:34 Jesus said to them, 'Knowledge of the mysteries of the kingdom of heaven has been granted to you….'Mt13:11 He taught them to pray.Cf.Lk11:1-2 He sent them out as his apprentices on mission;Cf.Lk10:1-20 he instructed them, 'Whoever wishes to come after me must deny himself, take up his cross, and follow me.'Mk8:34 To sustain them on their mission, Jesus promised to send them the Spirit of Truth, who would lead the Apostles to all Truth.Cf.Mt10:20;Jn16:13

Christ's [method] was multi-dimensional. It included his words, his signs, and the wonders he worked. He reached out to the poor, to sinners, and to those on the margins of society. He proclaimed insistently the coming of the Kingdom of God, the forgiveness of sins, and reconciliation with the Father. Especially in his parables, Christ invited his listeners to a whole new manner of life sustained by faith in God, encouraged by hope in the kingdom, and animated by love for God and neighbor. He used every resource at his disposal to accomplish his redemptive mission.

'The whole of Christ's life was a continual teaching:
his silences, his miracles, his gestures, his prayer,
his love for people, his special affection for the little
and the poor, his acceptance of the total sacrifice
on the Cross for the redemption of the world,
and his Resurrection are the actualization of his word
and the fulfillment of revelation.'CT9

Holy Spirit
(NDC, page 93)

The Holy Spirit unfolds the divine plan of salvation within the Church. With Christ, the Holy Spirit animates the Church and directs her mission. The Holy Spirit makes the Paschal Mystery of Christ present in the human mind to accept Christ, converts the human heart to love Christ, and encourages the human person to follow Christ. Thus, the Holy Spirit makes new life in Christ possible for the believers. 'The Holy Spirit, the artisan of God's works, is the master of prayer.'CCC741 The Holy Spirit draws all humanity to Christ and, through Christ, into communion with the Trinity.

reflection

1. D.T. Niles defined evangelization as "one beggar telling another beggar where to find food." How is evangelization always "new"

2. Is there any sort of "personal transformation" or "conversion" to which God may be calling me this week?

3. How might I name the response of my faith as itself a gift from God?

4. How would I summarize the "good news" of Jesus Christ?

5. To whom do I feel closest: to God the Father, God the Son, or God the Holy Spirit? How could I describe this closeness to a person who does not know God?

6. Most of the Nicene Creed (19 of 31 lines) is about the mystery of the person of Jesus Christ, fully God and fully human. How can I respond to his invitation to know him better?

7. Am I at peace with (or do I wrestle with) the Church's distinction between the deposit of faith, which does not change, and the development of doctrine (the language we use to articulate the deposit of faith) that happens through history?

8. In 1 Timothy 2:4, Saint Paul wrote of what we call God's universal salvific will, that all be saved. Am I reassured or challenged by this teaching?

closing prayer

Are there intercessions from the group?

Conclude with the Our Father,
then recite the Apostles' Creed:

I believe in God, the Father almighty,
creator of heaven and earth.

I believe in Jesus Christ, his only Son, our Lord.
He was conceived by the power of the Holy Spirit
and born of the Virgin Mary.
He suffered under Pontius Pilate,
was crucified, died, and was buried.
He descended to the dead.
On the third day he rose again.
He ascended into heaven,
and is seated at the right hand of the Father.
He will come again to judge the living and the dead.

I believe in the Holy Spirit,
the holy catholic Church,
the communion of saints,
the forgiveness of sins,
the resurrection of the body,
and the life everlasting. Amen.

Praise To The Lord

Praise to the Lord, the Almighty, the King of creation!
O my soul, praise the Lord, who is our health and
salvation!
Join the full throng;
Wake, harp and psalter and song;
Sound forth in glad adoration!

Praise to the Lord, the only one, the maker of heaven,
It is the Lord who made the earth, the seas and all in them.
Can we yet see
How our desire and need
Meet in our Lord's will and union.

Praise to the Lord,
who brings our work to prosper before us;
Who from the heavens sent rivers of mercy into us.
Ponder anew
What the almighty can do,
Who in divine love befriends us.

Praise to the Lord,
Oh let all that is in us sing praising!
All that has life and breath, come forth and with us
    sing praising!
Let the Amen
Sound from all people again;
Gladly sing worship and praising!

Text: from Nehemiah 9:6, Joachim Neander, 1679
          Translated by Catherine Winkworth, 1863, altered
          Verse 2 by Stephen Joseph Wolf, 2009
Music: LOBE DEN HERREN 14 14 47 8; Straslund Gesangbuch, 1665

2

THE CHURCH

Opening Prayer: The Nicene Creed (see page iv) all together.

A member of the group reads **Jeremiah 31:10-14,31-34**
while others read along in their Bibles.

A member of the group reads **Matthew 16:13-28**
while others read along in their Bibles.

Then group members take turns reading the background:
(NDC, page 93)

"From her very beginnings the Church, which 'in Christ, is in the nature of a Sacrament,' has lived her mission as a visible and actual continuation of the [teaching] of the Father and of the Son."GDC141 The Church constantly seeks to discover the most fruitful way to announce the Good News and looks first to the method used by God. The Church's proclamation of the Gospel has been both progressive and patient, as was her Master's, respecting the freedom of individuals and taking into consideration their "slowness to believe."EA29 In the lives and teachings of the martyrs and saints, in the treasury of her teaching, in the witness of catechists, and in various examples of Christian life, the Church has [sought to imitate God's own method] for communicating the faith... [Disciples] of Jesus today will [seek to] pass through the same process of discovery and commitment.

21

Human Experience
(NDC, page 98)

Jesus consistently used the ordinary human experiences of daily life to form his disciples, to point to the end of time, and to show the transcendent dimension of all of life and of God's eternal presence in it. Because the eternal Word assumed human nature, human experience is the *locus* for the manifestation and realization of salvation in him. By the grace of the Holy Spirit, persons come to know Christ, to know that he was sent from the Father, and to know that he died to save them in the midst of [our] human experience.

Human experience is affected by the fallen state of human nature; human beings are in need of redemption in Jesus Christ, and their experiences can lead to errors in judgment and action. However, human experience has been enlightened by Christ; for that reason, it can connect the person intimately with the Christian message.

Drawing by
Fr. Norman Fisher

*By grace you have been saved through faith,
and this is not from you; it is the gift of God.* Ephesians 2:8

Discipleship

The Christian faith is, above all, conversion to Jesus Christ, full adherence to his person and the decision to walk **in his footsteps**.Cf.GDC152   Discipleship is thus centered on the person of Jesus Christ and the kingdom he proclaims. 'By following the example of his self-giving love, we learn to be Christian disciples in our own time, place, and circumstances.'OH46   In learning to follow Christ, we become aware that there exist 'facets of Christian life that come to full expression only by means of development and growth toward Christian maturity.'CG20 For disciples, saying '*yes*' to Jesus Christ means that they abandon themselves to God and give loving assent to all that he has revealed.

Mary is the first disciple, a unique instrument of Revelation and a model for all disciples. From all eternity the Father chose her, a young Jewish woman of Nazareth in Galilee, to conceive within her body, by the power of the Holy Spirit, the human body of his divine Son. God prepared her by his grace to cooperate freely with his will and to share her humanity with the divine Savior for whom she and all Israel confidently hoped. The Blessed Virgin Mary, by a singular grace from God, was preserved from sin from the first moment of her own conception until the end of her earthly life. 'Most blessed among all women' Luke 1:42, Mary was 'full of grace' Luke 1:28 and was a fitting vessel in which the word of God became flesh. Her faith, her sinlessness, her perpetual virginity, and her divine motherhood converged to cooperate with God's will to make her the perfect disciple.

Children
(NDC, page 99)

It is notable that, while children do not have the capacity to understand and articulate the content of the faith in the same way as do adults, they have a unique ability to absorb and celebrate the most profound truths of the faith. Children with cognitive disabilities often have an unusual intuitive understanding of the sacred. God's self-revelation unfolds in children in extraordinary ways, and his grace often develops within them a deep spirituality that continues to grow as they mature. Children are capable of being formed as disciples of the Lord from an early age. Their ongoing formation, which includes learning the basic truths of the Christian faith, increases their capacity to understand and articulate those truths more deeply later in life and disposes them to live Christ's message more faithfully.

Christian Community
(NDC, page 100)

The Christian community is the context in which individuals undertake their journey in faith toward conversion to Christ and discipleship in his name.

For most people, the parish...is the door to participate in the ordinary Christian community. Therefore, 'it is the responsibility of pastors and laity to ensure that those doors are always open.'WJ6 It is the place...where the Christian faith deepens and where the Christian community is formed. In the parish the members of the Christian community 'become aware of being the **people of God**.'GDC257 In the parish the faithful are nurtured by the word of God and nourished by the sacraments, especially the Eucharist. From the parish the faithful are sent on their apostolic mission in the world. 'The parish is still a major point of reference for the Christian people, even for the non-practicing.'CT67

Family
(NDC, page 100-101)

The Christian family is ordinarily the first experience of the Christian community and the primary environment for growth in faith. Because it is the 'church of the home,' [the domestic church,]FC38 the family provides a unique *locus* for catechesis. It is a place in which the word of God is received and from which it is extended. Within the Christian family, parents are the primary educators in the faith and 'the first heralds of the faith with regard to their children.'LG11 But all the members make up the family, and each can make a unique contribution to creating the basic environment in which a sense of God's loving presence is awakened and faith in Jesus Christ is confessed, encouraged, and lived. Within the Christian family, the members first begin to learn the basic prayers of the tradition and to form their consciences in light of the teachings of Christ and the Church. *Family members learn more of the Christian life by observing each other's strengths [and] weaknesses than by formal instruction* [Emphasis added]. They learn *intermittently* rather than systematically, *occasionally* rather than in structured periods [Emphasis added]. Often extended family members take on a primary responsibility in transmitting the faith to the younger members. Their shared wisdom and experience often constitute a compelling Christian witness.

The Catechist
(NDC, page 101)

Under the guidance of the Holy Spirit, catechists powerfully influence those being catechized by their faithful proclamation of the Gospel of Jesus Christ and the transparent example of their Christian lives. [Effective]… catechists…fully [commit] to Jesus Christ. They…firmly believe in his Gospel and its power to transform lives….

Catechists [seek to] make the words of Christ their own: 'My teaching is not my own but is from the one who sent me,'Jn7:16 and they confess with St. Paul, 'I handed on to you . . . what I also received.'1Cor15:3

By Heart
(NDC, page 102-103)

'…Texts that are **memorized** must at the same time be taken in and gradually understood in depth, in order to become a source of Christian life on the personal level and the community level.'CT55 [Learning by heart is best used as] a process that, begun early, continues gradually, flexibly, and never slavishly. In this way, certain elements of the Catholic faith, tradition, and practice are learned for a lifetime, form a basis for communication, allow people to pray together in a common language, and contribute to the individual's continued growth in understanding and living the faith. Among those formulations [to] be learned by heart are…:

1. Prayers such as the Sign of the Cross; Lord's Prayer; Hail Mary; Apostles' Creed; Acts of Faith, Hope, and Charity; and the Act of Contrition.

2. Factual information contributing to an appreciation of the place of the word of God in the Church and the life of the Christian through an awareness and understanding of the key themes of the history of salvation; the major personalities of the Old and New Testaments; and certain biblical texts expressive of God's love and care.

3. Formulas providing factual information regarding the Church, worship, the church year, and major practices in the devotional life of Christians including the parts of the Mass, the...sacraments, the liturgical seasons, the holy days of obligation, the major feasts of our Lord and our Blessed Mother, the lives of the saints (especially those newly canonized or those special to particular regions), the corporal and spiritual works of mercy, the various Eucharistic devotions, the mysteries of the rosary..., and the Stations of the Cross.

4. Formulas and practices dealing with the moral life of Christians including the Ten Commandments, the Beatitudes, the gifts of the Holy Spirit, the theological and moral virtues, the precepts of the Church, the principles of Catholic social teaching, and the examination of conscience. cf.NCD176

In addition..., memorization of favorite psalms, songs, prayers, and poetry in praise of Christ our Savior is an effective form of catechesis that nourishes the human heart and helps to form the human spirit in Christ.

Commitment
(NDC, page 104)

Learning by Christian living is...learning by doing. ...[The] faithful actively respond to God's loving initiative through praying; celebrating the sacraments and the Liturgy; living the Christian life; fostering works of charity (meeting the immediate needs of those who are poor and vulnerable) and works of justice (working to address the injustices that exist in the systemic and institutional organizations of society); and promoting virtues from the natural law such as liberty, solidarity, justice, peace, and the protection of the created order. The participation of **adults** in their own catechetical formation is essential, since they have the fullest capacity to understand the truths of the faith and live the Christian life.

In the United States, Christian beliefs, practices, and values are often challenged by the dominant secular culture. The prevailing culture tends to trivialize, marginalize, or privatize the practice of religious faith. Both the private practice and the public witness of knowledgeable and committed Christians are indispensable factors in the sanctification of the world, a responsibility to which all the baptized are called. In such an environment, living an active Christian life becomes...crucial...

...[The] Church wisely and repeatedly insists that adult faith formation is 'essential to who we are and what we do as Church'TT43 and must be 'situated not at the periphery of the Church's educational mission but at its center.'NCD 40
OH 42

Apprenticeship

(NDC, page 104-105)

Learning by apprenticeship...links an experienced Christian believer, or mentor [or sponsor], with one who seeks a deeper relationship with Christ and the Church. ...

All catechesis includes more than instruction. 'It must be an integral Christian initiation.'CT21 Learning by apprenticeship ordinarily includes the profession of faith, education in the knowledge of the faith, celebration of the mysteries of the faith, practice of the Christian moral virtues, and dedication to the daily patterns of Christian prayer. It is a guided encounter with the entire Christian life, a journey toward conversion to Christ. It is a school for discipleship that promotes an authentic following of Christ based on the acceptance of one's baptismal responsibilities, the internalization of the word of God, and the transformation of the whole person to 'life in Christ.'

Knowledge of ourselves
is the necessary and only step by which
we can ascend to the knowledge and love of God.
St. Anthony

In your nature, O eternal Godhead,
I shall know my own nature.
St. Catherine of Siena

Amen, I say to you, unless you turn and become
like children, you will not enter the kingdom of heaven.
Matthew 18:3

29

Prayer
(NDC, page 111-12)

God draws every human being toward himself, and every human being desires communion with God. Prayer is the basis and expression of the vital and personal relationship of a human person with the living and true God: 'God tirelessly calls each person to **that mysterious encounter** known as prayer.'CCC2567 His initiative comes first; the human response...is itself prompted by the grace of the Holy Spirit. That human response is the free self-surrender to the incomprehensible mystery of God. In prayer, the Holy Spirit not only reveals the identity of the Triune God to human persons, but also reveals the identity of human persons to themselves. It has been expressed throughout the history of salvation in the words and actions of prayer.

Liturgical prayer is the participation of the People of God in Christ's work. 'Every liturgical celebration, because it is an action of Christ the Priest and of his Body, which is the Church, is a sacred action surpassing all others. No other action of the Church can equal its efficacy by the same title and to the same degree.'SC7 The sacraments, especially the Eucharist, are the Church's preeminent experiences of liturgical prayer.

'In the liturgy, all Christian prayer finds its source and goal.'CCC1073 The rhythms of prayer within the life of the Church are both liturgical and personal. Liturgical prayer is the public prayer of the Church. It is the work of Christ, and as such it is the work of the Church. Personal prayer is an essential aspect of the human person's relationship with God, which can find expression in and be nourished by various devotional prayers, such as the Holy Rosary, Stations of the Cross, and novenas.

Since the time of the apostles, the Church has abided by the exhortation 'to pray constantly.'1Th5:17 The Liturgy of the Hours, or the Divine Office, is the daily public prayer of the Church; in it 'the whole course of the day and night is made holy by the praise of God.'SC84 ... 'The laity, too, are encouraged to recite the divine office,... with priests, or among themselves, or even individually."SC100

The living Tradition of the Church, however, contains more than the great treasury of liturgical prayer. **Personal prayer** is God's gift to the 'humble and contrite heart.' Ps51:19 It expresses the covenant relationship that binds God to the person and the person to God. The connection is Christ, the Son of God made flesh. He is the new and eternal covenant whose blood 'will be shed on behalf of many for the forgiveness of sins'Mt26:28 so that humanity may be redeemed and restored to communion with God. Personal prayer expresses communion with the life of the Blessed Trinity. The Holy Spirit inspires hearts to pray, removes obstacles to living life in Christ, and leads humanity into communion with the Father and the Son. Personal prayer permeates the daily life of the Christian and disposes him or her toward liturgical, communal, or public prayer.

Where your treasure is, there also will your heart be.
Matthew 6:21 and Luke 12:34

The glory of God is the human person fully alive.
St. Irenaeus

reflection

1. The word "church" is from the Greek "ekklesia," for the Hebrew word for the "assembly" in the 40-year desert wandering, freed from slavery, still being led into the promised land. Theologians also speak of church as body of Christ, people of God, sacrament, communion, institution, servant, discipleship, visible society...
    What image of "church" do I find most helpful?

2. The word "disciple," meaning student and follower, is related to the word "discipline."
    To what kind of discipline is God calling me?

3. Is there anything about my faith that I wish I could better articulate? Can anyone suggest for me a book, film, course, web site, etc.?

4. Family members learn the faith intermittently and occasionally. How do I feel about my family learning the faith by observing my strengths and weaknesses? How's my family doing as a school of discipleship?

5. What scripture verses do I know by heart?
    Why these particular words?

6. In what primary ministry or apostolate has God called me to serve others? How is God also using this to form me as a Christian?

7. To which saint would I like to be an apprentice?
    What's keeping me from doing so?

8. What are the differences between liturgical prayer and personal prayer? What is my favorite way to pray?

closing prayer

Are there intercessions from the group?

Conclude with the Our Father,
then recite the Apostles' Creed:

I believe in God, the Father almighty,
creator of heaven and earth.

I believe in Jesus Christ, his only Son, our Lord.
He was conceived by the power of the Holy Spirit
and born of the Virgin Mary.
He suffered under Pontius Pilate,
was crucified, died, and was buried.
He descended to the dead.
On the third day he rose again.
He ascended into heaven,
and is seated at the right hand of the Father.
He will come again to judge the living and the dead.

I believe in the Holy Spirit,
the holy catholic Church,
the communion of saints,
the forgiveness of sins,
the resurrection of the body,
and the life everlasting. Amen.

Lord Who At Your Last Supper You Did Pray

Lord, who at your Last Supper you did pray
That all your Church might be forever one,
Grant us at ev'ry Eucharist to say
With longing heart and soul, "Your will be done."
O may we all one bread, one body be,
Through this blest Sacrament of Unity.

For all your Church, O Lord, we intercede;
Make all our sad divisions soon to cease;
Draw us the nearer each, to each we plead,
By drawing all to you, O Prince of Peace;
Thus may we all one bread, one body be,
Through this blest Sacrament of Unity.

We pray for all who wander from your fold;
O bring them home, Good Shepherd of the sheep,
Back to the faith which saints believed of old,
Back to the Church which still that faith does keep;
Soon may we all one bread, one body be,
Through this blest Sacrament of Unity.

So, Lord, at length when sacraments shall cease,
May we be one with all your Church above,
One with your saints in one unbroken peace,
One with your saints on one unbounded love;
More blessed still in peace and love to be
One with the Trinity in Unity.

Text: William H. Turton, 1859-1938, altered.
Music: UNDE ET MEMORES 10 10 10 10 10 10, William H. Monk, 1923-1899.

3

SACRAMENTS

Opening Prayer: The Nicene Creed (see page iv) all together.

A member of the group reads **Ephesians 4:1-16** while others read along in their Bibles.

A member of the group reads **Luke 5:12-26** while others read along in their Bibles.

Then group members take turns reading the background:
(NDC, page 113)

The liturgical life of the Church revolves around the sacraments, with the Eucharist at the center. 'The sacraments are efficacious signs of grace, instituted by Christ and entrusted to the Church,' by which divine life is given to us and celebrated.CCC1131... [The Church names seven sacraments: Baptism, Confirmation, Eucharist, Penance, Anointing of the Sick, Holy Orders, and Matrimony.]

R.C.I.A. (NDC, page 115)

[The process of Christian formation, known as the **Rite of Christian Initiation of Adults** consists normally of four stages, with rituals that mark them:]

[1] [**Inquiry**, or] pre-catechumenate, coincides with the first evangelization, in which the primary proclamation of the Gospel and [often an] initial call to conversion to Christ takes place [and many questions can be raised. Inquirers often proclaim the faith in profound and honest questions.]

[2] ...[**Catechumenate** begins with] the handing on of the Gospels...and begins the period [of] a more integral and systematic catechesis [for] the catechumens [those preparing for baptism] and candidates [those who are already baptized seeking to become Catholic.] [This period begins for most with the *Rite of Welcome* at a Sunday Mass.]

[3] ...**Purification and Enlightenment** [is celebrated with the *scrutinies* (prayers of blessing, normally on the 3rd, 4th and 5th Sundays of Lent),] by more intense prayer, and by the study and conferral of the Creed and the Lord's Prayer. [This time includes more serious proximate preparation for the sacraments of initiation.]

[4] ...**Mystagogy**, or post-baptismal catechesis, marks the time in which the neophyte experiences the sacraments and enters fully into the life of the community. Cf.RCIA9-40

...The baptismal catechumenate is both 'a process of formation and a true school of the faith,'GDC91 It is a fruitful blend of instruction and formation in the faith; it progresses through gradual stages; it unfolds the Church's rites, symbols, and biblical and liturgical signs; and it incorporates the catechumens into the Christian community of faith and worship. While mystagogical, or post-baptismal, catechesis should not slavishly imitate the structure of the baptismal catechumenate, it should recognize that the baptismal catechumenate provides an admirable model for the whole of the Church's catechetical efforts and especially emphasizes the necessity for lifelong catechesis. Cf. Synod of Bishops, *Message to the People of God* (October 27, 1977), 8.

Sacraments of Initiation
(NDC, page 118,121)

Christian initiation is celebrated in **Baptism**, **Confirmation**..., and **Eucharist**. ... Through these sacraments, a person is incorporated into the Church, is strengthened for participation in the Church's mission, and is welcomed to partake of the Body and Blood of Jesus Christ. ...

In the Eastern Churches, **Baptism**, **Chrismation**, and **Eucharist** are celebrated together in infancy, and their intimate relationship is apparent. While the Latin Church has separated the celebration of Baptism from Confirmation and Eucharist, she also recognizes their essential interconnection.

Baptism

1. [Baptism] is the foundation of the Christian life because it is the journey into Christ's death and Resurrection, which is the foundation of our hope.
2. [Baptism] gives sanctifying grace, that is, God's life.
3. [Baptism] gives...a new birth in which [we] become children of God, members of Christ, and temples of the Holy Spirit.
4. [Baptism] cleanses people from original sin and from all personal sins.
5. [Baptism] incorporates us into the life, practices, and mission of the Church.
6. [Baptism] imprints on [our] souls an indelible [mark or] character that consecrates [us] for Christian worship and is necessary for salvation in the case of all those who have heard the Gospel and have been able to ask for this sacrament.Cf.CCC1257

...[Through] Baptism we receive a share in the mission of Christ as **king, priest**, and **prophet**.

...Baptism 'symbolizes the catechumen's burial into Christ's death, from which he [or she] rises up by resurrection with him, as *a new creature.*'CCC1214

...Baptism is 'the basis of the whole Christian life, the gateway to life in the Spirit...and the door which gives access to the other sacraments.' CCC1213...

...[Through] Baptism the faithful 'share in the priesthood of Christ, in his prophetic and royal mission.' CCC1268

...[The] 'Most Holy Trinity gives the baptized sanctifying grace, the grace of *justification*' (thus 'the whole organism of the Christian's supernatural life has its root in baptism')

→ 'enabling them to believe in God, to hope in [God], and to love [God] through the theological virtues'

→ 'giving them the power to live and act under the prompting of the Holy Spirit through the gifts of the Holy Spirit'

→ 'allowing them to grow in goodness through the moral virtues'CCC1266

...[Having] 'become a member of the Church, the person baptized belongs no longer to himself [or herself], but to him who died and rose for us.'CCC1269...

...[The] ordinary minister for the Sacrament of Baptism is a priest or deacon...but...in the case of necessity, any person who intends to do what the Church does can baptize by pouring water on the candidate's head and saying the Trinitarian formula.

Together we confess: By grace alone, in faith in Christ's saving work and not because of any merit on our part, we are accepted by God and receive the Holy Spirit, who renews our hearts while equipping and calling us to good works

Joint Declaration on the Doctrine of Justification, The Lutheran World Federation and The Roman Catholic Church, 1999, in English, 2000, #15

Confirmation

(NDC, page 123)

...Confirmation increases and deepens the grace of Baptism, imprinting an indelible character [or mark] on the soul.

...Confirmation **strengthens** the baptismal conferral of the Holy Spirit on those confirmed in order to incorporate them more firmly in Christ, strengthen their bond with the Church, associate them more closely with the Church's mission, increase in them the gifts of the Holy Spirit CCC1303, and help them bear witness to the Christian faith in words and deeds...

[The basic symbols of the Rite of Confirmation are] the imposition of hands, the anointing with Sacred Chrism, and the words of the sacramental formula.... [The] bishop is the ordinary minister of...Confirmation. ...

Eucharist

(NDC, 123-25)

The Eucharist is the ritual, sacramental action of **giving thanks** and praise to the Father. It is the sacrificial memorial of Christ and his body, the Church, and is the continuing presence of Christ in his Word and in his Spirit.

In the Mass, or 'the Divine Liturgy' as it is termed in the Eastern Catholic Churches, the Eucharist constitutes the principal liturgical celebration of the Paschal Mystery of Christ and the ritual memorial of our communion in that mystery. Acting through the ministry of the priests, the bread and wine become—through Transubstantiation—Christ himself. Christ offers the Eucharistic sacrifice and is really present under the species of bread and wine.

['source and summit of the Christian life'LG11]

…[The Eucharist] is a sacred banquet in which the People of God share the benefits of the Paschal Mystery, renew the covenant that God has made through the blood of Christ, and anticipate the heavenly banquet.

…[This] work of salvation … is made present by the liturgical action that Christ himself offers…

…[The] Eucharist nourishes the Body of Christ, the Church, and each individual communicant….

…Christ is **present** whole and entire, God and man, substantially and permanently, and in a unique way under the species of bread and wine.RP1-2

…Christ is also present in his word, in the body of the faithful gathered in his name, and in the person of the priest who acts in the person of Christ, the Head of his Body, the Church.

…[The] effects of the sacrament [are] unity in the Body of Christ and provision of spiritual food for the Christian's journey through life.

…[Reception] of the Body and Blood of Christ signifies and effects communion with the most Holy Trinity, forgives venial sins, and, through the grace of the Holy Spirit, helps the communicant to avoid mortal sin.

…[Through] the power of the Holy Spirit, the Eucharist forms the Church.

…[In] the Eucharist, 'Christ associates his Church and all her members with his sacrifice of praise and thanksgiving offered once for all on the cross to his Father.'CCC1407…

…[Remembering that Jesus and his disciples were faithful Jews,] the Jewish roots of the Last Supper [are] the renewal of God's covenant with his people in the blood of his beloved Son.

...[The] essential signs of the Eucharistic sacrament are bread and wine, on which the power of the Holy Spirit is invoked and over which the priest pronounces the words of consecration spoken first by Jesus during the Last Supper.

...[The] '**bread and wine** are changed, a change traditionally and appropriately expressed by the word *Transubstantiation*, so that, while the appearances of bread and wine remain, the reality is the Body and Blood of Christ.' NCD121

...[The] Eucharist commits those who receive it to serve the poor.Cf.CCC1397

...[It] is the preeminent sign of the unity of the Church.

...[It] is an effective sign of the unity of all Christians... [One] day—that is, the Parousia—by the grace of the Holy Spirit, the divisions that separate Christians will be healed...

...[In the meantime, we pray for that healing unity while observing] guidelines for Eucharistic sharing...set forth by the...bishops. Cf. GRC

...[The] celebration of the Eucharist in the sacrifice of the Mass is the origin and consummation of the worship shown the Blessed Sacrament outside of Mass. cf.HC [The Blessed Sacrament is kept on reserve in the Tabernacle in parish churches, so that communion may be taken to the sick and homebound on Sundays and during the week. Devotional visits to the Blessed Sacrament are encouraged.]

...[Commonly called 'the Easter duty,' Catholics are to] receive Holy Communion at least once a year during the Easter season.

...[The faithful are encouraged to] receive Holy Communion when they participate in the celebration of the Eucharist [while free of grave sin].

...We are called to realize that we become what we receive [St. Augustine] — which has great implications for how we live and act.

bread taken, blessed, broken, and given [See Matthew 26:26]
*...where two or three are gathered together in my name,
there am I in the midst of them.* Matthew 18:20

Sacraments of Healing
(NDC, page 131)

[The Sacraments of Initiation help keep us aware of the redemptive sacrifice of Christ, reminding us of our need for conversion, penance, and forgiveness, because we] 'hold this treasure in earthen vessels.'2Cor4:7   This treasure of new life in Christ can be gradually squandered or lost entirely by sin.

But the Father's design for creation intends that all people be saved by Christ's self-sacrificial love.   [See 1 Timothy 2:4] Toward that end, Christ founded his Church to continue his work of healing and salvation through the power of the Holy Spirit. Immediately after he called his first disciples, Christ cured many who were sick with various diseases,Cf.Mk1:21-2:12 exorcised demons, cleansed lepers, and forgave the sins of a paralytic, restoring him to physical and spiritual health.   Christ's healing and reconciling ministry is carried on in the Church principally through the two sacraments of healing: the Sacrament of Penance and **Reconciliation** and the Sacrament of the **Anointing of the Sick**.

42

Reconciliation
(NDC, page 132-134)

[In addition to the term 'reconciliation,' the Catechism also calls this the Sacrament of Penance, Conversion, Confession, and Forgiveness. Cf.CCC1423-24]

On the evening of his Resurrection, Jesus sent his apostles out to reconcile sinners to his Father and commissioned them to forgive sins in his name: '*Peace be with you. As the Father has sent me, so I send you.* And when he had said this, he breathed on them and said to them, *Receive the holy Spirit. Whose sins you forgive are forgiven them, and whose sins you retain are retained.*' John20:21-23

Catechesis for the Sacrament of Reconciliation first depends on the person's acknowledgment of God's faithful love, of the existence of sin, of the capacity to commit sin, and of God's power to forgive sin and reconcile the sinner with himself and with the Church. *If we say, 'We are without sin,' we deceive ourselves, and the truth is not in us.* 1John1:8 ...

...[We have] a merciful and loving father who runs to greet the repentant sinner, throws his arms around him, and welcomes him home with a banquet.Cf.Luke15:11-32

...Christ, the Redeemer..., through the action of the Holy Spirit, pours himself out with a 'love more powerful than death, more powerful than sin.' RIM8

...Christ is at work giving actual graces in the sacrament, thereby effecting what the sacrament signifies, namely 'reconciliation with God by which the penitent recovers grace; reconciliation with the Church; remission of the eternal punishment incurred by mortal sins; remission, at least in part, of temporal punishments resulting from sin; peace and serenity of conscience, and spiritual consolation; and an increase of spiritual strength for the Christian battle.' CCC1496

...[The faithful are taught] 'to confess in kind and in number all serious sins committed after baptism and not yet directly remitted through the keys of the Church nor acknowledged in individual confession, of which [they are] conscious after diligent examination of conscience.' CICc.988.1

...[The] Sacrament of...Reconciliation consists of

> [1] repentance,
>
> [2] confession,
>
> [3] reparation on the part of the penitent, and
>
> [4] the priest's absolution.

...'[M]ortal sin is sin whose object is grave matter and which is also committed with full knowledge and deliberate consent.' RAP17

...[Priests] are bound by the seal of confession, under the most severe penalties,Cf.CIC,c.1388.1 to keep absolute secrecy regarding the sins that penitents have confessed to them.

...[The] Penitential Rite in the Eucharistic Liturgy [*Lord, have mercy; Christ, have mercy; Lord, have mercy*] is a means of repentance for venial sin [or]...'sin that merits merely temporal punishment' CICc.988.2 [though confession is recommended].

...[Faithful Christians are challenged] to recognize the presence of evil in the social order, to evaluate that evil in light of...Gospel values..., to accept appropriate individual and corporate responsibility, and to seek forgiveness for participation in social evil, or the evil of society.

...[Even] those who have 'put on Christ' Cf.Gal3:27 in the sacraments of initiation...are all sinners... [We remain in need of] conversion and forgiveness.

...[Christians are called] to grow in...awareness of their solidarity with other human beings, to seek forgiveness from them, and to offer forgiveness to them when necessary.

Anointing of the Sick
(NDC, page 136-37)

Jesus, the divine physician of our souls and bodies, is at work in the Sacrament of the Anointing of the Sick: touching our wounds in order to heal us and restoring us to communion with his Father in the Holy Spirit. Christ's personal solicitude for the sick is expressed in the words of James: *Is anyone among you sick? He should summon the presbyters of the church, and they should pray over him and anoint [him] with oil in the name of the Lord, and the prayer of faith will save the sick person, and the Lord will raise him up. If he has committed any sins, he will be forgiven.* James5:14-15

...Christians experience [solidarity with the suffering Christ] through their own illness—Christ was no stranger to the world of human suffering, for he took human suffering upon himself, voluntarily and innocently.
...[The "form" of the sacrament includes] the laying-on of hands, the anointing of the head and hands with blessed oil, and the words of the sacramental formula. Cf.CCC1519
...[Like] 'all the sacraments [it is] a liturgical and communal celebration, whether it takes place in the family home, a hospital or church, for a single sick person or a whole group of sick persons.'CCC1517
...[Any] baptized person who is seriously or chronically ill or in danger of death from advancing age may receive this sacrament, [not only those at the point of death]. SC73...

...[The] Anointing of the Sick is also a preparation for death, to be received by those [in their last days. It is usually best to call for a priest while the person is still aware; sooner is better than later.] ...[Integral] to the last rites...which Catholics value so highly, Anointing of the Sick, with the Sacrament of...[Reconciliation]...and the Eucharist as Viaticum [food for the journey, literally "on the way with], form the sacraments of departure. Cf.CCC1523,1525

...[A] person who has previously received the Sacrament of the Anointing of the Sick may receive it again if the condition worsens still or if the condition initially improves and then worsens again.

...[Those] preparing for serious surgery, the elderly whose infirmity declines further, and seriously ill children [are invited] to ask for sacramental anointing.

> Pastoral note: For many priests, a most convenient time for this sacrament is often after Sunday Eucharist.

...[While only bishops and priests are ministers of the Sacrament of the Anointing of the Sick, all]...members of the parish [are encouraged] to visit and care for the sick and express concern and love for them.

> Pastoral note: If a priest is unavailable in the final hours, the lay faithful may wish to offer the *Prayer of Commendation* from the *Rites for the Care of the Sick*:

Lay Minister, with hands joined:
Lord Jesus Christ, our Redeemer, we pray for your servant *N.*,
and commend *him/her* to your mercy.
For *his/her* sake you came down from heaven;
receive *him/her* now into the joy of your kingdom,
for though *he/she* has sinned,
he/she has not denied the Father, the Son, and the Holy Spirit,
but has believed in God and has worshipped *his/her* Creator.

All: Amen.

A Ritual For Laypersons,
The Liturgical Press, 1993, pg. 88.

reflection

1. The word "liturgy" means "the work of the people." What do I think this means?

2. The structure of the RCIA catechumenate (gather, proclaim, break open, and go forth), following the structure of the Eucharist, has influenced faith formation in the church, especially apparent in the Life Teen movement and small group faith sharing communities. How might this structure be used by my family or in my personal prayer?

3. How do I reconcile baptism as *necessary for salvation* with the Church's teaching on freedom of religion?

4. The gospel of Luke tells us of Jesus as an infant, as a twelve-year-old, and that Jesus began his ministry at about the age of 30. How would I tell a twelve-year-old that he or she is a priest, a prophet, and a royal? What difference does this make for us?

5. In the gospels of Mark and Luke, Jesus hears the voice from the clouds at his baptism. How would I tell a three-year-old that he or she is a beloved son or daughter of God, in whom God takes great delight?

6. How would I describe to an inquiring neighbor who is not Catholic the "real presence" of Christ the Risen Lord in the Eucharist?

7. The bishop, in our tradition the successor to the apostles and pastor of the of the "local church" (the diocese), is the ordinary minister of Confirmation. What do I remember about receiving the sacrament of Confirmation?

8. St. Augustine said, "Let your 'amen' be a 'yes' to your being part of the body of Christ." We say that "the Eucharist makes the Church." It is the "source and summit of the Christian life," the Church teaches. How do I experience the Sunday Eucharist? Does it change me?

9. At the Eucharist, Christ is present in the species of bread and wine, in the word of God proclaimed and heard, in the gathered assembly (Matthew 18:20), and in the person of the priest. How can being aware of these rich manifestations help me to prepare for Sunday Eucharist or the Viaticum?

10. G.K. Chesterton declared a saint is one who knows he or she is a sinner. *While we were still sinners Christ died for us* Romans 5:8; in the Exultet of the Easter Vigil the deacon sings: "O happy fault, O necessary sin of Adam, which gained for us so great a Redeemer!" What keeps people away from the sacrament of Reconciliation?

closing prayer

Are there intercessions from the group?

Conclude with the Our Father,
then recite the Apostles' Creed:

I believe in God, the Father almighty,
creator of heaven and earth.

I believe in Jesus Christ, his only Son, our Lord.
He was conceived by the power of the Holy Spirit
and born of the Virgin Mary.
He suffered under Pontius Pilate,
was crucified, died, and was buried.
He descended to the dead.
On the third day he rose again.
He ascended into heaven,
and is seated at the right hand of the Father.
He will come again to judge the living and the dead.

I believe in the Holy Spirit,
the holy catholic Church,
the communion of saints,
the forgiveness of sins,
the resurrection of the body,
and the life everlasting. Amen.

The King Of Love My Shepherd Is

Melody: *O Breathe On Me, O Breath of God...*

The King of Love my Shepherd is,
Whose goodness fails me never;
I nothing lack if I am his
And he is mine forever.

Where streams of living water flow,
My ransomed soul he leads me,
And where the verdant pastures grow,
With food celestial feeds me.

Perverse and foolish, I do stray,
But yet in love he seeks me
And on his shoulder gently laid
And home, rejoicing, brings me.

In death's dark vale I fear no ill,
With you, dear Lord, beside me;
Your rod and staff my comfort still,
Your cross before to guide me.

You spread a table in our sight,
Your unction grace bestowing;
And, oh! the transport of delight
With our cup overflowing.

And so through all the length of days
Your goodness fails us never.
Good Shepherd, may we sing your praise
Within your house forever!

Text: Psalm 23, Henry W. Baker, 1868, altered
Music: ST. COLUMBA, CM; Gaelic Folk Melody

4

VOCATION

Opening Prayer: The Nicene Creed (see page iv) all together.

A member of the group reads **Isaiah 61:10 - 62:5**
while others read along in their Bibles.

A member of the group reads **John 15:1-17**
while others read along in their Bibles.

Then group members take turns reading the background:
(NDC, page 139)

Holy Orders and **Matrimony** are the sacraments at the service of communion because they 'confer a particular mission in the Church and serve to build up the People of God.'CCC1534 The Eastern Catholic Churches call these the 'Mysteries of Vocation.'

Pastoral Note: We begin our lives as single people, each created uniquely in the image of God. Many stay single, (and a fair number discern this call by way of marriage and divorce). What does the Catholic catechism say about this vocation? Just that some forgo marriage in order to
(1) care for their parents or brothers and sisters,
(2) give themselves more completely to a profession,
(3) or serve other honorable ends. CCC 2231
A single Christian can stay grounded in **Baptism,**
Confirmation and **Eucharist** as his or her sacraments of vocation, commitment and communion.

51

Holy Orders

The whole Church is a priestly people and…through Baptism all the faithful share in the priesthood of Christ, the common priesthood of the faithful. Those who have been consecrated by the Sacraments of Baptism, Confirmation or Chrismation, and Eucharist share the vocation to holiness and to the mission of proclaiming the Gospel to all nations.Cf.CIC,c.1008 That call, issued by Jesus Christ, establishes the common priesthood of the faithful.

Within this common priesthood of the faithful, some are consecrated through the Sacrament of Holy Orders as members of the ministerial priesthood 'to nourish the Church with the word and grace of God.'LG11…

> '[Based] on this common priesthood and ordered to its service, there exists another participation in the mission of Christ: the ministry conferred by the Sacrament of Holy Orders, where the task is to serve in the name and in the person of Christ the Head in the midst of the community.'CCC1591…

> '[The] ministerial priesthood differs in essence from the common priesthood of the faithful because it confers a sacred power for the service of the faithful.'CCC1592

…[There] are three degrees of the ordained ministry: that of bishops, that of priests, and that of deacons.

The ministerial priesthood and the common priesthood of the faithful participate 'each in its own proper way, in the one priesthood of Christ.'CCC1547 Though they are ordered to each other, they differ essentially.Cf.LG10 The ministerial priesthood is at the service of the common priesthood of the faithful. …[The] Sacrament of Holy Orders 'is the sacrament through which the mission entrusted by Christ to his apostles continues to be exercised in the Church until the end of time.'CCC1536 ...

...[Bishops], priests, and deacons are called by Christ and, through sacramental ordination, are empowered to minister in his name and in the name of the Church.

...[As with Baptism and Confirmation, Ordination imprints an indelible sacramental character that marks one permanently.]

...[The] Rite of Ordination [includes] the laying-on of hands and the bishop's prayer of consecration....

...[Bishops], priests, and deacons...share in the saving action of Jesus Christ's ministry of teaching, sanctifying, and building up the Church.

...[The] Latin Church calls ordained ministers, with the exception of permanent deacons, to consecrate themselves with undivided heart to the Lord by committing themselves to celibacy as a sign of the new life of service to which they are consecrated; ordinarily, the Sacrament of Holy Orders is conferred only on men who freely promise to embrace celibacy for the length of their lives.Cf.CCC1579

...[In] the Eastern Churches, priests and deacons are ordinarily permitted to marry before their ordination.

...[Permanent] deacons may be men who are already married but..., after ordination to the [diaconate], they cannot enter into another marriage.

...[Religious life of sisters, brothers, monks and nuns] 'derives from the mystery of the Church'CCC926 and is 'distinguished from other forms of consecrated life by its liturgical character, public profession of the evangelical counsels' of poverty, chastity, and obedience; of 'fraternal life led in common'; and of 'witness given to the union of Christ with the Church.'CCC925

Marriage

(NDC, pages 142-43)

Christian marriage is the union of a baptized man and woman who freely enter into a loving covenant with each other in Christ. 'The matrimonial covenant, by which a man and a woman establish between themselves a partnership of the whole of life and which is ordered by its nature to the good of the spouses and the procreation and education of offspring, has been raised by Christ the Lord to the dignity of a sacrament between the baptized.' CIC,c.1055.1; cf. CCEO, c.776.1-2.

This self-giving love of husband and wife represents the mutual love of Christ for his bride, the Church, and the love of the Church for her bridegroom, Christ. 'Thus, the *marriage bond* has been established by God...in such a way that a marriage concluded and consummated between baptized persons can never be dissolved.'CCC1640 It gives permanent witness to the fidelity of love. 'This bond, which results from the free human act of the spouses and their consummation of the marriage, is a reality, henceforth irrevocable, and gives rise to a covenant guaranteed by God's fidelity. The Church does not have the power to contravene this disposition of divine wisdom.'CCC1640 ...

...[Marriage] is a distinct and dignified vocation in the Church.

...[The] effects of the Sacrament of [Marriage are] the establishment of a perpetual and exclusive bond between the spouses that is sealed by God himself,Cf.Mk10:9 the perfection of the mutually exclusive and permanent love of the couple, the strengthening of their indissoluble unity, and the experience of a foretaste of the Kingdom of God.

54

…[It] is in the love and struggles of marriage that a couple attains the holiness of their vocation.

…[The] unity of the couple [in Christian marriage] is a unity founded in an equal personal dignity and expressed in an unreserved mutuality of self-giving.

…[The] family is the first and essential center of faithful living, the domestic Church.

…[The] home is the first school of Christian life and human enrichment.

…[A] couple's marriage in Christ is a sacred relationship that is supported for the length of their lives by the grace to love each other with the love Christ has for the Church.

…**[F]idelity**, **Indissolubility**, and **Openness to children** are essential to Christian marriage [Emphasis added].

…[Christian] marriage is for the mutual support of the spouses, their growth in love, and the procreation and education of their children.

…[Parents have a] personal responsibility to protect the human life that they co-create with God from the moment of conception to natural death.

…[The] couple themselves are the ministers of the sacrament… [Their] consent should be publicly exchanged in their vows before a priest or deacon (or a witness authorized by the Church) and two other witnesses, ideally in the presence of an assembly of the faithful. … In Byzantine Catholic Churches, the priest is the minister of the sacrament [and] the vows are optional because the statement of the intention is made in a different manner.

Pastoral note: If a bride or groom is Catholic, the Church asks that the marriage be held within the Catholic "form": in a church, witnessed by a priest or deacon. A great gift of the Catholic form is the opportunity to hear from one priest or deacon how the Church understands the nature of the sacrament of marriage.

...[Those] preparing for ecumenical or [interfaith] marriages [will want to] discuss openly and honestly the challenges and opportunities that the respective faith traditions present for their relationship, the education and formation of their children, and the harmony of the family.... [A] marriage [in the Catholic form] between a baptized Catholic and a spouse baptized in another Christian tradition [is presumed to be a Sacrament].... [A marriage] between a baptized Catholic and an unbaptized person[, while non-sacramental, is still a marriage].

Pastoral note: The sacrament of marriage can be defined as when a baptized man and a baptized woman, who have a good sense of who they are, who have revealed themselves to each other, come together freely and, in freedom, exchange mutual consent to bond in permanence, fidelity, and openness to children. If either the man or the woman withholds (or is incapable of giving) even one of these three consents, the union remains a civil contract, but it is not the sacrament of marriage.

...[Those who suffer the trauma of divorce are due] the care and concern of the whole Christian community...

...[Divorced] persons and their children [remain and are to be welcomed] as truly integral members [of the parish].

...[The] fact of divorce itself does not prevent reception of the sacraments...

Pastoral note: Catholics who are divorced and remarried without having obtained a declaration of nullity are asked as a discipline to refrain in the meantime from receiving holy communion. This is a "discipline" within the Church, and has nothing to do with judgment or sin. Those who are faithful to this discipline can give a powerful witness to the value of the sacrament of marriage.

...[A] 'declaration of nullity' [,sometimes called an annulment,] is an official decision by the Church that a marriage was invalid from the beginning.... [A 'declaration of nullity'] does not affect [in any way] the legitimacy of children resulting from the union.

Pastoral note: When a "declaration of nullity" is granted, it does not mean that the couple was never married. There was a marriage, and there was a divorce. Rather, the process asks a basic question: "Was the marriage a sacrament?" If it was a sacrament, then it cannot be dissolved. If it was not a sacrament, then the formerly married man and woman are both free to enter into the sacrament. The process is often described as embarrassing, annoying, and healing.

...[Those] Catholics who are divorced and remarried outside the Church [remain members of the Body of Christ and are encouraged] 'to listen to the word of God, to attend the sacrifice of the Mass, to persevere in prayer, to contribute to works of charity and to community efforts in favor of justice, to bring up their children in the Christian faith, to cultivate the spirit and practice of penance and thus implore, day by day, God's grace.'FC84

...[And they are encouraged to seek to regularize their marriages, if possible.]

Pastoral note: Please, do not give up.

57

Creation in the Image and Likeness of God

(NDC, page 159)

The **dignity of human persons** is initially rooted in our creation by God in [God's own] image and likeness. The divine image is present in every person. The Father has created human beings in Christ, and in Christ we come to know ourselves and our exalted vocation....

Endowed with a spiritual and immortal soul, human beings are 'the only creatures on earth that God has wanted for [their] own sake.'GS24 By reason, we are capable of understanding the created order; by free will we are capable of directing our lives toward the good and away from evil. Yet we know how deeply these gifts have been wounded by original sin. Human beings also [share a call to seek and love] 'what is true and good.'GS15 From our conception, we are destined for eternal happiness. We have a desire for happiness that God has placed in our hearts...[, drawing us to God]. 'The beatitude of eternal life is a gratuitous gift of God. It is supernatural, as is the grace that leads us there.'CCC1727 Life in the Holy Spirit makes the fulfillment of this desire possible.

In Christ, God reveals how we human beings are to live our lives. God created [us] with the freedom to initiate and direct [our] own actions and to shape [our] own lives. '**Freedom** is the power, rooted in reason and will, to act or not to act, to do this or that, and so to perform deliberate actions on one's own responsibility.'CCC1731 Freedom makes human beings responsible for their actions to the extent that they are voluntary. Every human person is a free and responsible agent with an inalienable right to exercise freedom, especially in moral and religious matters. In fact, action is human action insofar as it is free.

This human freedom does not, however, entitle the person to say or do just anything. Human beings are not fully self-sufficient. We are capable of sin. Yet Christ redeemed us from the sin that held us in bondage and set us free. As St. Paul said, 'For freedom Christ set us free." Gal5:1

Human freedom, therefore, is the capacity to choose good or evil. The more one chooses to do what is good, the more free one becomes. The choice to do evil, on the other hand, is an abuse of freedom and leads to the 'slavery of sin.'Rom6:17 In Christ, human beings freely direct themselves to life in the Holy Spirit. 'Where the Spirit of the Lord is, there is freedom.'2Cor3:17 Freely choosing to do the good, to obey the universal and unchanging moral norms, in no way diminishes the freedom and dignity of the human person. *'The Crucified Christ reveals the authentic meaning of freedom; he lives it fully in the total gift of himself* and calls his disciples to share in his freedom.'VS85

Drawing by Fr. Norman Fisher

Another definition of freedom from the saints:
The capacity to say to God, as in Mary's "fiat," only "Yes!"

Challenges to the Dignity
of the Human Person

(NDC, pages 160-62)

Although religious faith is a strong force in the lives of many [in the United States, our] country's dominant secular culture often contradicts the values on which this nation was established. There is a tendency to privatize religious faith, to push its considerations to the margins of society and to banish its concerns from the public conversation in which social policy is formed.

At the center of the moral vision contained in this nation's founding documents are two basic principles:

(1) the recognition of the dignity and rights of the human person as endowed by the Creator and

(2) liberty and justice for all.

While the people of the United States can rightly be proud of what we have achieved in pursuing those noble principles, unfortunately they are sometimes contradicted in practice and even in law.

In a society that publicly proclaims that life is an inalienable right and affirms the value of life, the inherent dignity and incomparable value of every human person is being threatened: 'The very right to life is being denied or trampled upon, especially at the more significant moments of existence: the moment of birth and the moment of death.'EV18 Abortion and euthanasia directly attack innocent life itself, the most fundamental human right and the basis for all other rights. They attack the weakest and most defenseless members of society, the unborn and the sick. 'Such direct attacks on human life, once crimes, are today legitimized by governments sworn to protect the weak and marginalized.'LGL5

Without the benefit of carefully considered ethical analysis, some current biological and technological developments undermine the dignity of the human person and even attempt to create human life itself by artificial means.

In addition, the treatment of immigrants, of illegal aliens, of those in prison, and of criminals and their victims must be shaped by this recognition of the inherent dignity of every human person.

> The new evangelization calls for followers of Christ who are unconditionally pro-life: who will proclaim, celebrate and serve the **Gospel of life** in every situation. A sign of hope is the increasing recognition that the dignity of human life must never be taken away, even in the case of someone who has done great evil. Modern society has the means of protecting itself, without definitively denying criminals the chance to reform. I renew the appeal I made most recently at Christmas for a consensus to end the death penalty, which is both cruel and unnecessary.
>
> Pope John Paul II, Mass at St. Louis, Mo. (January 27, 1999)

In a society that publicly proclaims that liberty is an inalienable right, freedom has come to mean an unlimited individual autonomy in which many people find their ultimate sense of fulfillment in the exercise of unrestricted personal choice. Individual freedom becomes the absolute and the source of other values. Such an excessively individualistic notion of freedom distorts the true meaning of freedom, pits the individual person against society, and empties social life, even family life, of its significance. 'Yet between life itself and freedom there is an inseparable bond, a link. And that link is love or fidelity.'FL9

In a society that values power, utility, productivity, and profit, the helpless, the weak, and the poor are seen as liabilities. The unprecedented economic and military power of the United States has sometimes led to grave injustices both at home and abroad.

At home, it has fueled self-absorption, indifference and consumerist excess:

> Overconfidence in our power, made even more pronounced by advances in science and technology, has created the illusion of a life without natural boundaries and actions without consequences. The standards of the marketplace, instead of being guided by sound morality, threaten to displace it. We are now witnessing the gradual restructuring of American culture according to the ideals of utility, productivity and cost-effectiveness. It is a culture where moral questions are submerged by a river of goods and services and where the misuse of marketing and public relations subverts public life. LGL3

The gradual erosion of the principles on which this country was founded contributes to a growing secularism, materialism, and an *'ethical relativism,* which would remove any sure moral reference point from political and social life.'VS101 In a secularist society there is a grave danger that people will live as if God did not exist. When the sense of God is lost, the sense of humanity is lost as well. In a materialist society there is a grave danger that people will begin to believe that they are what they have. 'In a widely dechristianized culture, the criteria employed by believers themselves in making judgments and decisions often appear extraneous or even contrary to those of the Gospel.'VS88 People wonder if they should hold any truths as sacred. ...'In turn, the systematic violation of the moral law, especially in the serious matter of respect for human life and its dignity, produces a kind of progressive darkening of the capacity to discern God's living and saving presence.'EV21

In general, Christian morality
Upholds the right to life
    from conception to natural death,
teaches that human freedom reaches its authentic
    goal in love of the weak and defenseless
    and in defense of their rights,
Promotes the public expression of the Christian
    faith in the formation of social policy,
Helps the faithful to make practical moral decisions
    in the light of the Gospel,
and understands that power, wealth, utility, and
    productivity must be subordinated to and
    guided by higher moral values.

reflection

1. The 2002 North American Congress on Vocations called the Church to foster a "Vocation Culture," where we ask with regularity, and help one another to ask, the vocation question: "What is God calling me to do" today, in this situation, this year, with my life? What difference would a "culture of vocation" make?

2. All the baptized share in the common priesthood of the faithful, while it is the ordained priest who is empowered to hear confessions, grant absolution, and administer the anointing of the sick. How is forgiveness of a family member, neighbor, or co-worker a priestly act?

3. The ordained priesthood and the common priesthood of the faithful "are ordered to each other," but "differ in essence." How would I describe this to a neighbor who is the pastor of a non-Catholic congregation?

4. The sacrament of Marriage is conferred on the man and the woman by each other in their mutual exchange of consent. Their baptism empowers them to be ministers of marriage; in their self-giving love, they are the sacramental presence of Christ to each other. How can we help the Church to better support marriages?

5. Can I name circumstances in our culture which might challenge or limit the freedom of a couple seeking to enter into marriage?

6. Single, married, consecrated religious, or ordained, is it possible to attain holiness without struggling in life? Do I know anyone who has?

7. A member in my extended family has stopped going to Sunday Eucharist because he or she is recently divorced. What do I say?

8. How might I talk to a teen who fears he or she is "ugly" (or one I overhear calling another "ugly") about the dignity of being created in the image of God?

9. What is it about the way Jesus of Nazareth lived that speaks most eloquently about how God is calling me to live?

10. Right to life questions include abortion, euthanasia, the death penalty, dealing with embryos, the poor, unjust wages, migrant workers, access to health care, genocide, some wars, etc.
    Do any of these have my attention?
    How can I help integrate them as one consistent gospel of life?

11. What "higher moral values" would I like to see as guides to power, wealth, utility and productivity?

closing prayer

Are there intercessions from the group?

Conclude with the Our Father,
then recite the Apostles' Creed (see page 49).

O Breathe On Me O Breath Of God

Melody: *The King Of Love My Shepherd Is…*

O breathe on me, O breath of God,
Fill me with life anew,
That I may love what you have loved,
And do what you would do.

O breathe on me, O breath of God,
Until my heart is pure,
Until with you I will one will,
To do and to endure.

O breathe on me, O breath of God,
Inspire my busy mind,
Until this earthly part of me
Glows with your fire divine.

O breathe on me, O breath of God,
My soul shall never die,
But live in your eternal life,
Your love, the reason why.

Text: Edwin Hatch, 1878, altered
Music: ST. COLUMBA, CM; Gaelic Folk Melody

5

MORAL FORMATION IN CHRIST

Opening Prayer: The Nicene Creed (see page iv) all together.

A member of the group reads   **Ezekiel 36:22-28**
while others read along in their Bibles.

A member of the group reads   **Luke 4:1-13**
while others read along in their Bibles.

Then group members take turns reading the background:
(NDC, page 163)

Christ is the **norm** of morality. 'Christian morality consists, in the simplicity of the Gospel, in *following Jesus Christ*, in abandoning oneself to him, in letting oneself be transformed by his grace and renewed by his mercy, gifts which come to us in the living communion of his Church.'
VS119

Christian moral formation involves a journey of interior transformation in light of Christ's Paschal Mystery, which brings about a deep personal conversion to Christ. Conversion to Christ involves confession of faith in him, adherence to his person and his teaching, following in his footsteps, taking on his attitudes, and surrendering the old self in order to take up the new self in Christ. 'The Sermon on the Mount [*Matthew 5-7*], in which Jesus takes up the Decalogue, and impresses upon it the spirit of the beatitudes, is an indispensable point of reference for the moral formation which is most necessary today.'GDC85

Grace
(NDC, page 163-164)

Grace conforms the Christian to Christ. It is God's free initiative, which only he can give. It enables us to give ourselves freely in response. Even our preparation for grace is itself a work of grace. It is the **free** and undeserved help that God gives us to, in turn, respond to his call to become his adopted children, partakers of the divine nature and of eternal life. Cf.CCC1996,Cf.JDDJ37-39 Sanctifying grace is a participation in God's own life that introduces us into the life of the Holy Trinity. Through the grace of Baptism, we are brought into union with the Father; we become members of Christ's Body; and we are joined to the Spirit of the Father and the Son in the Church.

Whoever is in Christ is a new creation:
the old things have passed away;
behold, new things have come.
And all this is from God,
who has reconciled us to himself through Christ..

2Corinthians 5:17-19

Virtue
(NDC, page 164)

Human beings are wounded by sin and need help to live morally good lives. Divine grace transforms human nature. It elevates and purifies virtue so that a person may lead a morally good life. Virtue is the **habit** of tending toward the good and choosing the good in the concrete actions of a person's life. This gift of grace can also take the form of the **cardinal virtues**:

(1) **prudence,**

(2) **justice,**

(3) **fortitude,** and

(4) **temperance,**

which dispose the person to live in harmony with God, with others, and with the whole created order. The virtuous person freely practices the good. By the grace of the Holy Spirit, the virtuous person consistently seeks communion with God and becomes like God.

This gift of grace takes the form of the **theological virtues** of

(1) **faith,**

(2) **hope,** and

(3) **charity.**

These virtues have God as their origin and object. They are the foundation of Christian moral living—life in Christ. They transform the human capacity to do good into a participation in the divine nature. By the virtue of faith, we believe in God—all he has revealed to us and all the Church proposes for belief. By the virtue of hope, we trust in God's promise of eternal life and his grace to deserve it. And by the virtue of charity, 'the bond of perfection,' Col3:14 we love God above all else and our neighbor as ourselves for love of God.

Formation of Conscience

(NDC, page 165)

Moral conscience is a person's '**most secret core and ... sanctuary.**' GS16 It 'is a judgment of reason whereby the human person recognizes the moral quality of a concrete act.'CCC1778 It bears witness to the truth and judges particular choices, decisions, and actions to be either good or evil. By the judgment of conscience, a person recognizes the prescriptions of the moral law. One's conscience obliges one to follow faithfully what one knows to be good.

The dignity of the human person implies and requires uprightness of moral conscience. While moral conscience reflects God's law written in the human heart, it needs to be formed and informed. The judgments it renders must be enlightened. The formation of a conscience is a lifelong task...[in which] the Word of God illumines the way.

The formation of conscience is influenced by many human factors, such as the person's age, intellectual capacity, psychological capacity, emotional maturity, family experience, and cultural and social conditions. But the example of Christ's life and his teaching are the norm in the formation of conscience. The person's relationship with Christ, expressed by frequent participation in the sacramental and prayer life of the Church, is the basis for formation of the Christian moral conscience.

Christ's gift of the Spirit of Truth to the Church also ensures that the Church's teachings are true and consequently are necessary in the formation of one's conscience. The Church is the indispensable guide to the complete richness of the teachings of Christ. Thus,

'Catholics should always measure their moral judgments by the Magisterium, given by Christ and the Holy Spirit to express Christ's teaching on moral questions and matters of belief and so enlighten personal conscience.'NCD190

One's conscience can make an erroneous judgment when one faces a moral decision. While a human being must always obey the certain judgment of conscience, conscience can be poorly informed or simply ignorant. Persons are responsible for ensuring that their consciences are well formed and that their actions are determined accordingly. If the poorly formed or ignorant conscience is the result of personal neglect in its formation, the individual is culpable for the choices that are made. If the moral decisions made are the result of poor conscience formation or ignorance for which the person is not responsible, the person is not culpable for the evil committed as a result. [Human experience when transformed] through grace is more than...human life development. It is growth 'into Christ.' Christians deepen their relationship with the Risen Lord, which draws them into the very heart of Christ. Therefore, the transformation of self to the authenticity of being made in the image of God becomes a graced happening and a lifelong commitment to live in freedom, self-assurance, joy, and love.

True happiness is communion with God,
not material, social, or political success.
NDC, page 167

71

Sin
(NDC, page 166)

Sin **wounds** the loving relationship that God has initiated with [God's own] creatures. It is an offense against God that turns the human heart away from his love. It wounds human nature and injures human solidarity. Our sinfulness is the object of God's great mercy, for which the Church continually prays.

Original sin is the first obstacle to life in Christ. It is the loss of the holiness and grace that Adam and Eve received from God. It is transmitted to every person, weakening human nature and leaving it subject to suffering and death. In this state one cannot consistently or persistently avoid personal sin.

Personal sin, whether mortal or venial, is committed by an individual. It is an offense against God, an act contrary to reason. Personal sin wounds human nature, harms the Christian community, and damages human solidarity. Because sin wounds, one needs to be both forgiven and healed of sin, a healing that needs to begin within the heart and soul of the sinner.

Mortal sin is a person's deliberate choice to do something seriously contrary to divine law. 'Mortal sin is sin whose object is grave matter and which is committed with full knowledge and deliberate consent.' Rite of Penance 12 ...

Venial sin is a less serious offense against God. It is the failure to observe the less serious matters of the moral law, or the failure to observe the moral law in grave matter, but without full knowledge or complete consent. It diminishes or wounds the divine life in the soul and impairs the sinner's relationship with God. The repetition of individual acts of sin can lead one into a state of sinfulness. In addition, repetitive, deliberate, and unrepentant venial sin can lead to mortal sin.

Pastoral note: ***Sin:*** *an abuse of freedom given me by God.*
It is a sin if   *(1) it is wrong, and*
                   (2) I know it is wrong, and
                   (3) I freely do it (or omit it).

The Human Community
(NDC, page 168-69)

The model for the human community is the Holy Trinity: the unity of Father, Son, and Holy Spirit. The very nature of the Trinity is communal and social. 'God reveals himself to us as one who is not alone, but rather as one who is relational, one who is Trinity. Therefore, we who are made in God's image share this communal, **social nature**. We are called to reach out and to build relationships of love and justice.'scs1 The relationships that men and women are to establish among ourselves resemble the relationships between and among the divine persons within the Triune God. Those human relationships transcend the boundaries of language, race, ethnicity, gender, culture, and nation to bind people together in one human family. Every single member of that one human family is of inestimable worth, since each is made in the image of God and was created to be happy with God for all eternity.

People are social by nature. We need other people, and we need to live in society. The family, the community, and the state are the essential social contexts for the development of individual human beings. Ideally these social units bind people together by a principle of unity that goes beyond each individual. They are necessary structures within which human beings develop their individual potential and collaborate on the achievement of objectives that could not be accomplished by any single person. But these social structures can also present dangers. They can threaten personal freedom and exploit individual ability. The human person 'is and ... ought to be the beginning, the subject and the object of every social organization.' GS25

The fact that human beings are social by nature forms a fundamental tenet of Catholic social teaching. Since societies are essential to human development, and all human beings are called to communion with God, the way societies contribute to or impede [communion with God] involves profound moral questions. Societies are organized around certain social, political, economic, and legal principles—whether clearly articulated or not—and societies function within the institutions and structures that those principles initiate. 'Catholic social teaching provides principles by which the Church as an institution, and Christians as individuals, can evaluate political, economic, social, and legal structures.' NCD158

Society ought to promote the exercise of virtue, not obstruct it. Catholic social teaching recognizes a hierarchy of values within human society that 'subordinates ...material and instinctive dimensions to...interior and spiritual ones.' CA36 Since it is composed of human beings made in God's image and called to communion with him, human society ought to be primarily ordered to the spiritual dimension of the human persons who constitute it. Respect for the inherent dignity of every human person is the foundation of a just society, and its ultimate end is the development of those persons to their fullest potential. [Human] persons cannot be viewed merely as the means to a productive and profitable society. Rather, they should be seen as the architects and beneficiaries of the society that they have conceived and built.

Can we name basic human rights?
This list is from Pope John XXIII:
the right to live, food, clothing, shelter, medical care, rest, to be respected, education, to be able to worship God, to choose the kind of life one finds appealing, to work and exercise personal initiative, a wage sufficient to allow a family a standard of living consistent with human dignity, private property subject to a social obligation, to form associations, freedom of movement, to be active in public life. Peace On Earth (*Pacem in Terris*),
Pope John XXIII, 1963, #11-27

*[Humanity, the human person in solidarity, is]...
the author, center, and goal of all economic and social life.
The decisive point of the social question is that
goods created by God for everyone should in fact reach everyone
in accordance with justice and with the help of charity.*
Catechism of the Catholic Church, para. 2459

*The demands of justice must be satisfied first of all;
that which is already due in justice
is not to be offered as a gift of charity.*
Decree On The Apostolate Of Lay People
(*Apostolicam Actuositatem*), Vatican II, 1965, #8

*Not to enable the poor to share in our goods
is to steal from them and deprive them of life.
The goods we possess are not ours, but theirs.*
St. John Chrysostom

75

Moral Conversion & Society
(NDC, page 170)

Christian morality has a distinctly social dimension that derives from both the nature of the human person and the Church's social mission. The Christian person simply cannot live in society without recognizing the duties and responsibilities that naturally arise within that relationship. Our faith in the sovereignty of God and the destiny of the human person compels us to work for justice, to serve those in need, to seek peace, and to defend the life, dignity, and rights of every person.

> '**Catholics are called by God
> to protect human life,
> to promote human dignity,
> to defend those who are poor,
> and to seek the common good.**

This social mission of the Church belongs to all of us.
It is an essential part of what it is to be a believer.' EC1

We are called to be **leaven** in society, applying Christian values to every aspect of our lives. Our society needs the witness of Christians who take the social demands of the Gospel seriously and who actively practice the virtue of social justice. Christians, [whose identity is rooted in Baptism, are called to be] the 'servant' leaders that Jesus Christ challenged the first disciples to be…. [It] is 'the right and duty of Catholics and all citizens to seek the truth with sincerity and to promote and defend, by legitimate means, moral truths concerning society, justice, freedom, respect for human life and the other rights of the person…' CPL6

Catholic Social Teaching
(NDC, page 170-71)

The call to work for **social justice** is imbedded in the Gospel message of Jesus Christ, who came 'to bring good tidings to the poor / ...liberty to captives / and recovery of sight to the blind.'Lk4:18 That call has been further specified by the official teachings of the Church. The Church's social teaching comprises a body of doctrine, but it is not merely a series of documents. Rather, it is a living tradition of thought and action. This teaching is a

> call to **conscience, compassion**, and **creative action** in a world confronting the terrible tragedy of wide-spread abortion, the haunting reality of hunger and homelessness, and the evil of continuing prejudice and poverty. [It] lifts up the moral and human dimensions of major public issues, examining the **'signs of the times'** through the values of the Scriptures, the teaching of the Church, and the experience of the People of God. CST3

The Church's social doctrine is part of a systematic moral framework that includes the totality of Christ's moral teachings and those proposed by the Church in his name. The Church's social teachings are deeply integrated in her comprehensive vision of Christian morality. They cannot be treated as if they were peripheral or optional. They are constituent elements of her Magisterium, and the values on which they are based are indispensible components of life in Christ.

The Church's social teaching seeks to apply the Gospel command of love to and within social systems, structures, and institutions. It 'proposes principles for reflection; it provides criteria for judgment; it gives guidelines for action.'CCC2423 [The U.S. bishops] have articulated seven key themes that form the heart of Catholic social teaching:

(1) life and dignity of the human person;

(2) call to family, community, and participation;

(3) rights and responsibilities;

(4) the option for the poor and vulnerable;

(5) the dignity of work and the rights of workers;

(6) solidarity; and

(7) care for God's creation. SCS4-6

Visit www.usccb.org

Social Sin
(NDC, page 171-172)

The Church's emphasis on the social dimension of morality has led to the development of the concept of social sin. The **effect of sin over time** in society that causes society to create structures of sin is, by analogy, called 'social sin.' Personal sin expressed in the structures of society—personal sin that has social implications—is social sin. Social sin resembles original sin because it can exist in structures, because we can participate in an evil not of our own creation, and because it is sometimes the inheritance of our families and communities. Sinful structures set up social relationships that in turn cause systematic denial or abuse of the rights of certain groups or individuals. Organized social injustice, institutionalized racism, systemic economic exploitation, and the destruction of the environment are examples of the social consequences of sin.

Social sin can affect large numbers of people, yet it is very difficult to hold individuals accountable for it. Social injustice can be so deeply rooted and ingrained into the life of a society that it almost defies eradication. But individual persons are moral agents—structures or systems are not moral agents. Individuals devise structures and systems; individual people are responsible for the evil consequences of systematic social injustice and should work with others to change those structures and systems that cause evil.

Nobody has a right to be bored; there's too much to do.
Dorothy Day

The Decalogue
(NDC, page 173-181)

1. **I, the Lord, am your God. You shall not have other gods besides me.**

Catechesis on the first commandment awakens belief in God, inspires hope in him, and encourages believers to love him above all else. …

2. **You shall not take the name of the Lord, your God, in vain.**

…[The] second commandment encourages recognition of a sense of the sacred in life. …

3. **Remember to keep holy the sabbath day.**

…[C]reatures and their Creator are bound together in a loving relationship…[Creatures] owe their Creator worship and praise. On Sunday, the faithful are also asked 'to abstain from those works and affairs which hinder the worship to be rendered to God, the joy proper to the Lord's Day, or the suitable relaxation of mind and body.' CIC1247 …

4. **Honor your father and your mother.**

…[The] family is a communion of persons and a sign and image of the communion of the Father and the Son and the Holy Spirit.
…[The] family is 'the sanctuary of life,' EV6 'the vital cell of society,'AA11 and the church of the home. Cf.LG11 …

5. **You shall not kill.**

…[The] fifth commandment fosters respect for human life and an understanding of the sacredness of human life. …

6. You shall not commit adultery.

…[Human] sexuality [is a gift of] inherent goodness. …

7. You shall not steal.

…['Theft'] is taking goods, property, or time against the will of their legitimate owner. …
…[Stealing], vandalism, and fraud are violations of the rights of people to their property.

8. You shall not bear false witness against your neighbor.

…[God] is the source of all truth and…the fullness of truth is revealed in the person of Jesus Christ.
…[The] 'gravity of a lie is measured against the nature of the truth which it deforms, the circumstances, the intentions of the one who lies, and the harm suffered by its victims.' CCC2484
…[One] must repair the damage one has caused by lies.
…[The] right to the truth has certain limits.

9. You shall not covet your neighbor's wife.

…[The] proper place of [the gift of human sexuality] is within the context of a faithful, fruitful, and lifelong marriage.

10. You shall not covet anything that belongs to your neighbor.

…[The] 'goods of creation are destined for the entire human race' CCC2452 and…[we are all called to] respect… the integrity of creation and…to protect and preserve the environment for future generations.

The Beatitudes
(NDC, 183, 182)

Blessed are the poor in spirit,
  for theirs is the kingdom of heaven.

Blessed are those who mourn,
  for they shall be comforted.

Blessed are the meek,
  for they will inherit the land.

Blessed are they who hunger and thirst
for righteousness,
  for they will be satisfied.

Blessed are the merciful,
  for they will be shown mercy.

Blessed are the clean of heart,
  for they will see God.

Blessed are the peacemakers,
  for they will be called children of God.

Blessed are they who are persecuted for
the sake of righteousness,
  for theirs is the kingdom of heaven. Mt 5:3-10

The Ten Commandments and the Beatitudes describe the paths that lead to the Kingdom of God. Just as the Ten Commandments were at the heart of the Mosaic Law, the Beatitudes are at **the heart** of Jesus' preaching. They fulfill the promises God made to the chosen people and teach the people of the new covenant the final end to which God calls us, the Kingdom of Heaven. They reflect the desire for happiness that is written upon the human heart and reveal the goal of human existence, eternal happiness in communion with God.

> The Beatitudes depict the countenance of Jesus Christ and portray his charity. They express the vocation of the faithful associated with the glory of his Passion and Resurrection; they shed light on the actions and attitudes characteristic of the Christian life; they are the paradoxical promises that sustain hope in the midst of tribulations; they proclaim the blessings and rewards already secured, however dimly, for Christ's disciples; they have begun in the lives of the Virgin Mary and all the saints. CCC1717

...['All] people seek happiness: life, peace, joy, wholeness... of being.' NCD100

...[The] happiness which all people seek and for which they were created is given in Jesus.

...[The Beatitudes give] hope in time of difficulty.

...[They challenge] the Christian with decisive moral choices.

reflection

1. Our moral code helps us to do the good and avoid evil, teaches us what is good, helps us stay out of trouble, and helps to prepare us for the sudden or gradual conversion to which Christ is leading us. Is there a piece of our moral code that I had to learn the hard way?

2. Grace is a totally unmerited, totally free gift from God. Can I name the role of God's grace in my life?

3. The cardinal virtues (prudence, justice, fortitude, and temperance), also called the moral virtues and the human virtues, are given to us at birth, are formed with use, and are transformed by God's grace. What think I about the idea of virtue as a "habit?"

4. The phrase "let your conscience be your guide" is not permission to do whatever I want. Rather, my conscience is my taskmaster, calling me to the good. Why is it so important for the human person to form well his or her own conscience? Where do I go for help in this?

5. First Reconciliation is offered to children in the 2nd grade, the age of 7 being generally seen as the "age of reason." How would I describe to a 7 year old the difference between "mortal" and "venial" sin?

6. How does sin harm my relationship with God, with other people, with all humanity, and with myself?

7. How is our call (to protect human life, promote human dignity, defend the poor, and seek the common good) essential to what it is to be a believer?

8. Do I find it easier to pray with the 10 commandments or with the 8 beatitudes? Why do I think this is?

closing prayer

Are there intercessions from the group?

Conclude with the Our Father,
then recite the Apostles' Creed:

I believe in God, the Father almighty,
creator of heaven and earth.

I believe in Jesus Christ, his only Son, our Lord.
He was conceived by the power of the Holy Spirit
and born of the Virgin Mary.
He suffered under Pontius Pilate,
was crucified, died, and was buried.
He descended to the dead.
On the third day he rose again.
He ascended into heaven,
and is seated at the right hand of the Father.
He will come again to judge the living and the dead.

I believe in the Holy Spirit,
the holy catholic Church,
the communion of saints,
the forgiveness of sins,
the resurrection of the body,
and the life everlasting. Amen.

On This Day O Beautiful Mother

Refrain:

On_ this day, O beautiful Mother,
On_ this day we give you our love.
Near you, Madonna, fondly we hover,
Trusting your gentle care_ to prove.

Verse 1

On this day we ask to share,
Dearest Mother, your sweet care;
Help us 'lest our feet_ astray_
Wander from your guiding way.

Refrain

Verse 2

Queen of angels, deign to hear
Lisping children's humble pray'r;
Young hearts gain, O Vir_-gin pure_,
Sweetly to yourself allure.

Refrain

Text: Louis Lambillotte, SJ, 1796-1855, altered
Music: BEAUTIFUL MOTHER 77 77, Rohr's *Favorite Catholic Melodies*, 1857

6

THE SACRED

Opening Prayer: The Nicene Creed (see page iv) all together.

A member of the group reads   **Isaiah 2:2-5**
while others read along in their Bibles.

A member of the group reads   **Mark 12:13-27**
while others read along in their Bibles.

Then group members take turns reading the background:

Sacred Time: The Liturgical Year
(NDC, page 145-147)

'In Christianity time has a fundamental importance.' TMA10
Christ inaugurates 'the last days'TMA10,citing Heb1:2 and the
time of the Church that extends to the definitive coming of
the Kingdom of God in Jesus Christ. *'In Jesus Christ, the
Word made flesh, time becomes a dimension of God,* who is
himself eternal.'TMA10 Because of God's presence in time in
the person of Jesus Christ, time is sacred. Christians mark
time itself in relation to Christ.

The Latin Church lives and celebrates the mystery of
Christ in the span of a calendar year that re-presents the
mystery of the incarnation and redemption beginning with
the First Sunday of **Advent** [which is always the Sunday nearest to
November 30, the Feast of St. Andrew] and concluding on the

87

Solemnity of Christ the King. The Eastern Catholic Churches begin and end the liturgical year in accord with their particular traditions and follow the pattern of the Church year by means of their own particular lectionaries.

The economy or history of salvation unfolds throughout the liturgical year. Each day of the liturgical year is sanctified primarily by Christ's presence in it, but also by the prayer and the liturgical celebrations of the People of God, especially by the Mass and the Divine Office. The liturgical year exerts 'a special sacramental power and influence which strengthens Christian life.' MRNM

Season of	Season of		Season of	Season of	
ADVENT →	CHRISTMAS →	ORDINARY →	LENT →	EASTER →	ORDINARY
		Time			Time
VIOLET	WHITE	GREEN	VIOLET	WHITE	GREEN

From the time of the apostles, beginning with the actual day of Christ's Resurrection, the Church has celebrated the Paschal Mystery every first day, **Sunday**, the Lord's Day. 'The intimate bond between Sunday and the Resurrection of the Lord is strongly emphasized by all the Churches of the East and West.'DD19 Sunday is the weekly Easter. The day of Christ's Resurrection is both the first day of the week in the new creation and the 'eighth day' of the week, the image of eternity, which anticipates the glorious return of Christ and the fulfillment of God's reign. In the Byzantine Liturgy, Sunday is called 'the day that knows no evening.'

'The weekdays extend and develop the Sunday celebration.'NCD144 As the Church celebrates the mystery of Christ throughout the liturgical year, she honors [as first among the saints] Mary, the Mother of God, and Mother of the Church, who is 'inseparably linked with her son's saving work. In her the Church admires and exalts the most excellent fruit of redemption, and joyfully contemplates, as in a faultless image, that which she herself desires and hopes wholly to be.' SC103 The Church also commemorates the lives of the apostles, martyrs, and other saints, for they have been glorified with Christ. They are heroic examples of Christian life and intercede for the faithful on earth.

The liturgical year is divided into seasons that correspond to the major events in the history of salvation in Christ. The **Christmas** season celebrates the birth of the Savior in the mystery of the incarnation. In the Eastern Churches, after the close of the Christmas cycle, the Baptism of the Lord, called the 'Theophany,' is celebrated with great solemnity. Christ's baptism is seen as the paradigm or model for our own baptism.

For all the baptized, **Lent** is likewise the time to deepen and renew our own baptismal commitment. It is the primary penitential season in the Church's liturgical year, during which the faithful embrace the traditional practices of fasting, prayer, and almsgiving in preparation to renew their baptismal promises on Easter. These expressions of penance and self-denial manifest the Christian's continual need for conversion. Lent reflects the forty days that Jesus spent in the desert in fasting and prayer. It is also the time when the Church journeys with her catechumens and draws them toward the celebration of the Paschal Mystery in the final stages of their Christian initiation.

The **Easter** Triduum [of three days] celebrates the Lord's passion, death, and Resurrection and is the culmination of the entire liturgical year. The Easter Vigil marks the sacramental initiation of the catechumens into God's own life and the life of the Church. The Easter season extends for fifty days to the celebration of **Pentecost**, which commemorates the mission of the Holy Spirit from the Father and the Son to the Church.

In the Latin Church, **Ordinary Time**, which spans the periods from Christmas to Lent and from Pentecost through the Feast of Christ the King, celebrates different aspects of the fullness of the mystery of Christ from week to week. The Eastern Catholic Churches do not designate a season of Ordinary Time, but some dedicate a season to the power of the cross, beginning with the Feast of the Holy Cross, in which the cross is celebrated with great solemnity as the standard for Christian living as the believers await the second coming of Christ.

Sacred Art
(NDC, page 148-49)

In sacred art human hands express the infinite beauty of God and prompt praise and thanks. '*Sacred art* is **true and beautiful** when its form corresponds to its particular vocation: evoking and glorifying, in faith and adoration, the transcendent mystery of God—the surpassing invisible beauty of truth and love visible in Christ.'CCC2502 While the particular expressions of sacred art vary from culture to culture, authentic sacred art turns human minds, hearts, and souls toward God. 'Art is meant to bring the divine to the human world, to the level of the senses, then, from the spiritual insight gained from the senses and the stirring of the emotions, to raise the human world to God, to his inexpressible kingdom of mystery, beauty and life.' APC Sacred art 'should be worthy, becoming, and beautiful, signs and symbols of things supernatural.'SC122

Sacred art also has both a liturgical and catechetical purpose. Sacred art expresses the reverence and honor that are due the sacred. It conveys faith and fosters the expression of faith in the Liturgy. Sacramental celebrations depend on signs, symbols, and gestures to effect the grace they signify. Sacred art forms an essential part of the sacred Liturgy; it is 'integral to the Church at prayer because these objects and actions are [sacred] "signs and symbols of the supernatural world" and expressions of the divine presence.'BLS146 Whether traditional or contemporary, sacred art is suitable for religious worship as long as it expresses the divine in the midst of the human and leads to prayer.

Especially in the Eastern Churches, the liturgical **icon** portrays the sacred images of Christ, the Mother of God, the saints, or the angels. These icons represent various aspects of the mystery of the incarnation of the Son of God. 'Christian iconography expresses in images the same Gospel message that Scripture communicates by words. Image and word illuminate each other.'CCC1160 In Eastern spirituality, iconography depicts redeemed creation as a manifestation of the Divine Creator. Sacred images of the Mother of God, the angels, and the saints signify Christ, who is glorified in them. These sacred images can lead the faithful to contemplate the mystery they depict, to meditate on the Word of God, and to enter more deeply into communion with God.

Sacred Architecture
(NDC, page149)

In sacred architecture, the Church 'demonstrates God's reign over all space by dedicating buildings to house the Church and its worship.'BLS20 Christians build churches to worship God, but churches are not simply gathering spaces for the Christian assembly. Rather, 'the church building is a sign and reminder of the **immanence** and **transcendence** of God—who chose to dwell among us and whose presence cannot be contained or limited to any single place.'BLS50 A church is the house of God, his dwelling with those who have been reconciled to him by Christ and united to him by the Holy Spirit. A church building signifies the Church, the Body of Christ, alive in a particular place and among a particular people. It is the building in which the Christian community gathers to hear the word of God, to celebrate the Eucharist, to receive the sacraments, and to pray. It must have a place of great honor for God to dwell and for the faithful to pray. It should be a place appropriate for the reservation of the Eucharist and befitting the adoration of the Blessed Sacrament. It should be a form of worship itself, lifting the hearts and minds of the people to give praise and thanks to God. A church also signifies the Father's house, toward which his people journey and for which his people long. It should be easily accessible to all. The church building, in short, is a 'sign of the pilgrim Church on earth and reflects the Church dwelling in heaven.' RDC,ch.1,no.2

Sacred Music

(NDC, page 150-51)

Because sacred music gives glory and praise to God, it has been an integral part of the life of the Church from the very beginning. **Jesus sang** hymns with his apostles at the Last Supper,Cf.Mk14:26 and the first Christian writers attested to the customary inclusion of sacred music even in the earliest forms of Eucharistic Liturgy. Sacred music can be sung or performed on instruments. It can take a variety of forms, such as chant or polyphony, and can be ancient, medieval, modern or contemporary. 'Among the many signs and symbols used by the Church to celebrate its faith, music is of preeminent importance.'MC23

Thus, sacred music forms an integral part of the Church's Liturgy. More than just hymns, sacred music especially includes the Mass parts, so as to enrich the people's active participation in the Liturgy. It exhibits a 'certain holy sincerity of form'MS4 and performs a ministerial role in the celebration of divine worship. It serves—but does not dominate. …

In the Roman Liturgy, 'Gregorian chant holds pride of place.'GIRM41 Along with it, polyphony in particular is allowed, and other forms of sacred music as well, 'provided that they correspond to the spirit of liturgical action and that they foster the participation of all the faithful.' GIRM41 It is also desirable that everywhere the faithful 'know how to sing together at least some parts of the Ordinary of the Mass in Latin...set to the simpler melodies.' GIRM41

...Sacred music invites the faithful to give glory to God; it enhances [our] prayer, fosters the unity of [our] minds and hearts, and aims to draw [us] closer to Christ. Sacred music 'should assist the assembled believers to express and share the gift of faith that is written within them and to nourish and strengthen their interior commitment of faith.' MC23   Within the scope of sacred music, special attention should be given 'to the *songs used by the assembly*, since singing is a particularly apt way to express a joyful heart, accentuating the solemnity of the celebration and fostering the sense of a common faith and a shared love.' DD50

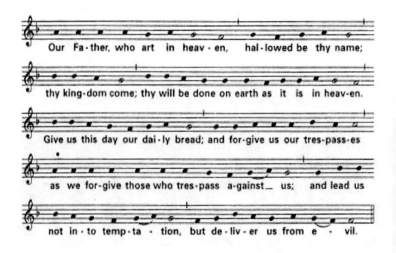

Our Fa-ther, who art in heav-en, hal-lowed be thy name;
thy king-dom come; thy will be done on earth as it is in heav-en.
Give us this day our dai-ly bread; and for-give us our tres-pass-es
as we for-give those who tres-pass a-gainst us; and lead us
not in-to temp-ta-tion, but de-liv-er us from e-vil.

Sacramentals
(NDC, page 151-52)

Sacramentals 'are sacred signs which bear a **resemblance to the sacraments...**' SC60 ...

Sacramentals are instituted by the Church in order to sanctify certain ministries, certain states of life, and certain objects Christians use in their daily lives. Sacramentals are often concrete examples of the inculturation of the faith [when] they express the faith in the particular language, customs, and traditions of a specific culture. 'They always include a prayer, often accompanied by a specific sign, such as the laying on of hands, the sign of the cross, or the sprinkling of holy water (which recalls Baptism).' CCC1668

Blessings of persons, meals, occasions, objects, and places are the most important kinds of sacramentals.Cf..*Book of Blessings* (New York: Catholic Book Publishing Co.,1989). Certain blessings consecrate persons to God, such as the abbot or abbess of a monastery, virgins or widows, and the members of vowed communities. Other blessings designate persons for ministry in the Church, such as catechists, [readers, altar servers,] and so forth. Still other blessings consecrate objects for liturgical use. Thus, the church building, the altar, the baptistry, oils to be used in celebrating the sacraments, sacred vessels, vestments, holy water, crosses and crucifixes, rosaries, palms, ashes, candles, medals, and various types of religious art and artifacts are all sacramentals. Some cultures have emphasized particular sacramentals; the faith has been inculturated through them.

Popular Piety & Devotion
(NDC, page 152-53)

Especially in light of the cultural, ethnic, and religious diversity of the United States, popular piety is a vital element in Catholic life that is expressed in a wide variety of popular devotions, such as various forms of prayers for the souls in purgatory, the use of sacramentals, and pilgrimages to shrines of Christ, the Blessed Virgin Mary, and the saints.Cf.EA16 In the United States, popular piety is a mode of the inculturation of the faith that is deeply rooted in the many cultures represented in its population. All racial, ethnic, and cultural groups have devotional practices that spring from their particular expressions of the one faith. Popular piety and the popular devotion it inspires provide many opportunities to encounter Christ in the particular circumstances of ethnic, cultural, and religious customs. If popular piety

'is well oriented, above all, by a pedagogy of evangelization, it is rich in values. It manifests a thirst for God which only the simple and poor can know. It makes people capable of generosity and sacrifice even to the point of heroism, when it is a question of manifesting belief.' EN48

The large and growing number of immigrants in the United States requires careful attention to the role of popular piety in many people's lives.TN31 This is true, for example, in the lives of Catholics whose roots are in Africa. The Church 'recognizes that it must approach these Americans from within their own culture, taking seriously the spiritual and human riches of that culture which appear in the way they worship, their sense of joy and solidarity, their language and their traditions.'EA16 As another example, [so many] Hispanics/Latinos'...view all of life as sacred and have generally developed a profound sense of the divine in daily living. This is evident in their popular religiosity'... In small communities, [they] find support to retrieve this sense of popular piety and to re-affirm the values contained in these celebrations.' USCCB, *Communion and Mission: A Guide for Bishops and Pastoral Leaders on Small Church Communities*, 1995,5

[Many] Asian and Pacific Catholic Americans and immigrants sustain their faith through devotional prayers and practices. They 'migrated with the experience and sensibilities of the great religions and spiritual traditions of the world...together with Christianity. Their experience of the great religions and spiritual traditions teaches them to live with profound presence of the sacred, a holistic approach to life and salvation, and spirituality adapted to their needs and a life-giving vitality.AP15 They 'bring popular devotions from their homelands and share them with fellow parishioners.'AP16

In the Latin Church in the United States, the Blessed Sacrament, the Sacred Heart, the Blessed Virgin Mary, and many saints are very important in popular devotion. 'Hispanic/Latino spirituality,' for example, 'places strong emphasis on the humanity of Jesus, especially when he appears weak and suffering, as in the crib and in his passion and death.... The Blessed Virgin Mary, especially under the titles of Our Lady of Guadalupe (Mexico), Our Lady of Providence (Puerto Rico), and Our Lady of Charity (Cuba), occupies a privileged place in Hispanic/ Latino popular piety.'HP12

African Americans likewise weave the message of evangelization into the cultural environment of their distinctive spirituality. The roots of African American spirituality are found in the family and issue from their history and lived experience. Their art, music, language, dance, and drama—as well as those of other Black cultures —should be incorporated into liturgical celebrations that are always "authentically black . . . truly Catholic . . . well-prepared and well-executed.'WW31 The Kingship of Jesus Christ, the pouring of libations, and an emphasis on Mary as the 'Great Mother' are a few examples of popular devotion that express the profound biblical themes of freedom and hope that are so integral to African American culture and spirituality.

Marian Devotion
(NDC, page 154-55)

Devotion to the Blessed Virgin Mary deserves special attention because it is such an important part of worship in the United States. The United States of America is under the patronage of the Immaculate Conception. ...Catholic people of all cultures have a deep love for the Mother of God. They employ many different expressions of that love to show the one faith that characterizes their particular prayer life and spirituality.

In this country, as well as throughout the world, the Rosary holds a place of honor as the most popular prayer devotion to the Blessed Virgin Mary. ...Pope John Paul II called for a renewed focus on the Rosary...[suggesting five new 'Luminous Mysteries' on the public life of Jesus].

...[The] various forms of popular devotion radiate from the Church's sacramental life but do not replace it.

Life In Christ
(NDC, page 157-58)

What the Christian faith confesses, the Christian sacraments celebrate and the Christian life animates. Christ calls his disciples in every age to live lives 'worthy of the gospel.' Phil 1:27   We are enabled to do so by the Father's love, the grace of Christ, and the gifts of the Holy Spirit that are diffused through the Church. The Christian moral life is living the call to holiness through transformation in Christ. …

The discipleship to which he has called all believers costs personally and dearly; the Gospel demands love and self-surrender. The way of Christ is the way of his cross: 'If anyone wishes to come after me, he must deny himself and take up his cross daily and follow me.'Luke 9:23 From the cross of Christ flows the water of life. The way of Christ leads to life.

reflection

1. The lack of enough time may be the universal poverty of our culture. What use of my time do I treat as sacred?

2. How is Sunday treated in my household as "the weekly Easter"?

3. Which art form would I use to show how the seasons of Advent, Christmas, Ordinary Time, Lent and Easter mirror the life and mission of Jesus Christ?

4. Can I name a particular work of sacred art that has both fed my soul in liturgy and given understanding to my faith?

5. God is both immanent (intimately near) and transcendent (beyond human senses and imagination). How can art, architecture and music help a faithful Christian live in this paradox?

6. Jesus sang hymns with his apostles at the Last Supper; why do they say Catholics can't sing?

7. Is there a sacramental that God has used to help form my faith? How?

8. Is there a devotional practice of a culture different from my own which I would like to learn about?

9. Thinking of a saint as one who is in heaven; calling to mind someone I have known, who has gone before us to heaven marked with the sign of faith; just as I could ask him or her to pray for me when that person walked the face of the earth, since in death life is changed, not ended, I can still ask him or her to pray to God for me; just so with Mary and all the saints: Which saint do I most often ask to pray for me? For those I love?

10. Do I know yet the name of my cross?

11. How do I experience Christ as my Risen Lord?

12. As I grow in understanding of my faith, to what specific loving actions do I sense God calling me?

closing prayer

Are there intercessions from the group?

Conclude with the Our Father,
then recite the Apostles' Creed:

I believe in God, the Father almighty,
creator of heaven and earth.

I believe in Jesus Christ, his only Son, our Lord.
He was conceived by the power of the Holy Spirit
and born of the Virgin Mary.
He suffered under Pontius Pilate,
was crucified, died, and was buried.
He descended to the dead.
On the third day he rose again.
He ascended into heaven,
and is seated at the right hand of the Father.
He will come again to judge the living and the dead.

I believe in the Holy Spirit,
the holy catholic Church,
the communion of saints,
the forgiveness of sins,
the resurrection of the body,
and the life everlasting. Amen.

footnote references

NDC *National Directory for Catechesis*, USCCB (Washington, D.C., 2005).

AP *Asian and Pacific Presence: Harmony in Faith*, USCCB (Washington, D.C., 2001)

APC Address to the Pontifical Commission for Sacred Art in Italy, Pope Paul VI, December 17, 1969.

BLS *Built of Living Stones: Art, Architecture, and Worship,* USCCB (Washington, D.C., 2000)

CCC *Catechism of the Catholic Church*, 2nd Edition, (Washington, D.C.: USCCB-Libreria Editrice Vaticana, 2000).

CCEO *Code of Canons of the Eastern Churches.*

CG *Called and Gifted for the Third Millennium*, USCCB, (Washington, D.C., 1995)

CIC *Code of Canon Law, Latin-English Edition, New English Translation,* Canon Law Society of America (Washington, D.C., 1999).

CL *The Vocation and Mission of the Lay Faithful in the Church and in the World* (Christifideles Laici), Pope John Paul II, 1988.

CPL *Doctrinal Note on Some Questions Concerning the Participation of Catholics in Political Life*, Congregation for the Doctrine of the Faith (Washington, D.C.: USCCB, 2004).

CST *A Century of Social Teaching: A Common Heritage, a Continuing Challenge*, USCCB, (Washington, D.C., 1991)

CT *On Catechesis in Our Time* (Catechesi Tradendae), Pope John Paul II, 1979

DD *Keeping the Lord's Day Holy* (Dies Domini), Pope John Paul II, 1998.

DV *Dogmatic Constitution on Divine Revelation* (Dei Verbum), Second Vatican Council, 1965.

EA *The Church in America* (Ecclesia in America), Pope John Paul II, 1999.

EC *Everyday Christianity: To Hunger and Thirst for Justice*, USCCB (Washington, D.C., 1998)

EN *On Evangelization in the Modern World* (Evangelii Nuntiandi), Pope Paul VI, 1975.

EV *The Gospel of Life* (Evangelium Vitae), Pope John Paul II, 1995.

FC *On the Family* (Familiaris Consortio), Pope John Paul II, 1981.

FL *Faithful for Life: A Moral Reflection*, USCCB (Washington, D.C., 1995)

102

footnote references, continued

GDC *General Directory for Catechesis*, Congregation for the Clergy
(Washington, D.C., USCCB, 1998).

GIRM *General Instruction of the Roman Missal,* (2001) (Washington,
D.C.: USCCB, 2003).

GMD *Go and Make Disciples: A National Plan and Strategy for
Catholic Evangelization in the United States* (Tenth Anniversary
Edition) USCCB (Washington, D.C., USCCB, 2002).

GRC *Guidelines for the Reception of Communion,* USCCB, November 14, 1996.

GS *Pastoral Constitution on the Church in the Modern World*
(Gaudium et Spes), Second Vatican Council, 1965.

HC *Holy Communion and Worship of the Eucharist Outside of Mass,*
Sacred Congregation for Divine Worship, 1973.

HP *The Hispanic Presence: Challenge and Commitment,*
USCCB, 1983.

JDDJ Catholic Church and Lutheran World Federation, *Joint Declaration on the Doctrine of Justification*, www.vatican.va, 1999.

JP *The Jewish People and Their Scriptures in the Christian Bible,*
Pontifical Biblical Commission (Vatican City: Libreria Editrice
Vaticana,2002), Section II.

LG *Dogmatic Constitution on the Church* (Lumen Gentium) Second
Vatican Council, 1964.

LGL *Living the Gospel of Life*, USCCB, 1998.

MC *Music in Catholic Worship*, rev. ed., USCCB, 1983.

MRNM *Maxima Redemptionis Nostra Mysteriis,* Sacred Congregation
of Rites, 1955.

MS *Instruction on Music in the Liturgy* (Musicam Sacram)
Congregation for Divine Worship and Discipline of the
Sacraments, in Flannery.

NCD *National Catechetical Directory* (Sharing the Light of Faith),
USCC, 1977.

NDCBI *National Directory for Catechesis Bulletin Insert* USCCB
Committee on Catechesis (Washington, D.C., 2005).

OH *Our Hearts Were Burning Within Us: A Pastoral Plan for Adult
Faith Formation in the United States*, USCCB
(Washington, D.C., 1999).

PT *Peace on Earth* (Pacem in Terris), Pope John XXIII, 1963.

RAP *Reconciliation and Penance* (Reconciliatio et Paenitentia), Pope
John Paul II, USCCB (Washington, D.C., 1984).

footnote references, continued

RDC *Rite of Dedication of a Church and an Altar,* Congregation for
the Sacraments and Divine Worship, 1978.

RIM *Rich in Mercy* (Dives in Misericordia), Pope John Paul II
(Vatican City), 1980.

RM *On the Permanent Validity of the Church's Missionary Mandate*
(Redemptoris Missio), Pope John Paul II, 1990.

RP *The Real Presence of Jesus Christ in the Sacrament of the
Eucharist: Basic Questions and Answers,* USCCB
(Washington, D.C., 2001).

SCS *Sharing Catholic Social Teaching: Challenges and Directions,*
USCCB (Washington, D.C., 1998).

SC *Constitution on the Sacred Liturgy* (Sacrosanctum Concilium)
Second Vatican Council, 1963.

SD Cf. Pope John Paul II, *Opening Address at Santo Domingo,* 1992.

TMA *On the Coming of the Third Millenium* (Tertio Millennio
Adveniente), Pope John Paul II, USCCB (Washington, D.C., 1994).

TN *Together a New People: Pastoral Statement on Migrants and
Refugees,* USCCB (Washington, D.C., 1986).

TT *To Teach As Jesus Did: A Pastoral Message on Catholic
Education,* USCC (Washington, D.C., 1972).

VS *The Splendor of Truth* (Veritatis Splendor),
Pope John Paul II, 1993.

WJ *Welcome and Justice for Persons with Disabilities,* USCCB
(Washington, D.C., 1999).

WW *What We Have Seen and Heard,* USCCB (Washington, D.C., 1984).

topic index